Telling the Story

RICHARD A. JENSEN

Telling the Story

Variety and Imagination in Preaching

AUGSBURG Publishing House • Minneapolis

TELLING THE STORY

Copyright © 1980 Augsburg Publishing House

Library of Congress Catalog Card No. 79-54113

International Standard Book No. 0-8066-1766-7

Scripture quotations unless otherwise noted are from the Revised Standard Version of the Bible, copyright 1946, 1952, and 1971 by the Division of Christian Education of the National Council of Churches.

MANUFACTURED IN THE UNITED STATES OF AMERICA

CONTENTS

INTRODUCTION

THE TASK OF PREACHING is a wonderful and frightful venture. But what exactly is that task? What does it mean to preach? What are we supposed to be doing when we climb the pulpit steps, read a passage from Scripture and then go on talking to the assembled congregation for the next fifteen minutes or so? *What shall we think about the task of preaching?* That is essentially the question that this work seeks to deal with. There are many ways in which the art and task of preaching has been described in the past. I am going to present and discuss three possible descriptions which I shall call *types of preaching.*

What I wish to share with you about preaching types comes from the perspective of a systematic theologian. That's an important factor for you to be aware of in reading this book. I am not trained as a homiletician, I do not teach homiletics and I have not been able to immerse myself in any significant way in the excellent literature produced by my colleagues working in the field of homiletics.

My interest is in types of preaching. Preaching, of course, is related to biblical and systematic theology. One's idea of the task of preaching rests on biblical and theological assumptions. The way we understand the Bible affects our preaching. Homiletics cannot be unrelated to biblical and theological assumptions and foundations. In my work as a theologian and preacher I have given a good deal of thought to the movement from these biblical and theological foundations to the various types of sermons. The conclusions I present here represent the present stage of my personal search for the connections between theology and types of preaching.

One word of explanation is in order here. Though I do not devote a separate section of this book to the matter, I presuppose that preaching is rooted deeply in specific texts of Scripture. Preaching is the proclamation of specific biblical texts. The content of preaching centers on the God who became flesh in Jesus Christ. Preaching is, by definition, the preaching of Christ, the announcement of the marvelously good news (gospel) that God calls outcasts, sinners and aliens into his kingdom. The reader should be aware of these presuppositions.

The format of what follows is quite simple. I will present three types of preaching. These types have emerged in my mind as I have preached and listened to preaching and gone about my theological business. I call these types, "Didactic Preaching," "Proclamatory Preaching," and "Story Preaching." "Didactic Preaching" appears to me to be by far the dominant type of preaching in our contemporary world. I hope to raise some serious questions about this particular type and the predominance of its usage. "Proclamatory Preaching," a type I have derived from the "new hermeneutic," Martin Luther and others, will be set forth as the type most suitable for our regular preaching routine. "Story Preaching" is my attempt to describe a *new* type which I believe is rooted in the character of the Bible and which may hold exciting potential for the future. "Story Preaching" is my creative contribution to the area of homiletics. I expect much more to be written about this type of preaching in the future.

The chapter on each preaching type will attempt to trace out the influences on my own thought in my particular way of describing these types. Each of these chapters will include a summary of the characteristics I would associate with the various types. Following each chapter which presents the preaching types will be a chapter containing a sermon(s) which illustrates that particular type of preaching.

It should be made perfectly clear at the outset that it is impossible to reduce all preaching to three types. I live under no illusion that I have finally discovered the secret and can definitively pass on to you *the three sermon types* that exist. That is not my purpose. I have isolated three types in a way that appears to be helpful for me and has proven useful to others as well. But these types are *neither definitive nor exhaustive*. They do not necessarily contradict each other. Though I will discuss them separately it is possible that these or any other sermon types necessarily intermingle in any given sermon.

My experience in preaching and in talking to others who preach is that we all tend to get stuck with one type or model of preaching. We have at our disposal only one set of conceptual tools as we think about the way the task of preaching should be accomplished. A fundamental goal of this book is to stimulate you to think about preaching in a variety of ways. I have become increasingly convinced that we as preachers must prepare our sermons in a variety of formats. I am convinced of that as much from the vantage point of the preacher as I am from the vantage point of the listener. Studies in human communication are telling us that people learn and hear differently; they receive communication in different ways. One person follows a logical argument best. Another needs verbal pictures to enhance communication. Still others do not get the message at all if their emotive instincts are not involved.

Preaching, therefore, ought to take a variety of forms. If this book helps to promote variety in your preaching it will have achieved its fundamental purpose. You may conclude that the types of preaching I develop in this book make no sense at all. In the process of thinking through what I have said, however, and in coming to your own conclusions about preaching you may develop new types and possibilities of telling the story. So be it! In whatever ways it happens I believe that all of us need a wider range of imagination as we approach the task of preaching. You are invited to come along with me now to see if together we can break open new vistas in our traditional patterns of thinking about preaching.

Finally, a word of sincere thanks to students, colleagues and pastors who have heard parts of the material in this book in earlier stages of its development. Without their words of encouragement, appreciation and constructive criticism I would not have had the courage to share my homiletical musings with a wider audience.

RICHARD A. JENSEN
Dubuque, Iowa

1

DIDACTIC PREACHING

THE FIRST TYPE OF PREACHING we shall discuss is what I have called didactic preaching. The word didactic means teaching. We will basically be discussing *preaching as teaching*. Teaching here is understood to be the communication of ideas, the making of points, an exchange of information, etc. Ninety percent of the preaching I hear and probably ninety percent of the preaching that I have done is essentially didactic in character.

That my preaching or the preaching of others was fundamentally didactic is a fact that I have come to realize quite gradually over the course of the recent years. The most formative influence in making me realize that what I was hearing from pulpits was didactic preaching has been the work of Marshall McLuhan.

McLuhan published his most influential works on the nature of our new mass electric media while serving as the Director of the Center for Culture and Technology at the University of Toronto. His name and his basic ideas have become familiar enough in our culture that his name can be used as an adjective ("McLuhanesque") in order to describe a particular phenomenon. His basic theses about culture, media and changing modes of human sensory perception have been widely debated. It is not my purpose in this place to become a partner to that debate. I would simply like to indicate that through my own studies in culture and media over the years I have become firmly convinced that the essential insights of McLuhan's work are correct. I find myself very much in debt to McLuhan in my own understandings of much that surrounds us in our culture.

I am fully aware that one could examine didactic preaching from a variety of viewpoints and listening stations. What I intend to do at this point, therefore, is to give a brief description of McLuhan's analysis of culture and try to unfold for you how my journey through that material has informed my thinking about "didactic preaching."

The Gutenberg Galaxy

Students interested in culture and mass media often ask where they should start reading in order to understand Marshall McLuhan. A good beginning point is McLuhan's, *The Gutenberg Galaxy*. Reading that book is an arduous task. It is well worth the effort, however, because most of the lighter, McLuhanesque treatments of his ideas *(The Medium Is the Massage, War and Peace in the Global Village* e.g.), are spin-offs of the basic ideas generated in *The Gutenberg Galaxy.*

In *Galaxy* McLuhan divides human history into several periods. These periods are characterized by him according to the senses (sight, taste, hearing, touch, smell) which dominate and stimulate life and learning. Earliest human life was life in a world dominated by the sense of *hearing.*

It was a world in which the ear was the paramount sense for accumulating the knowledge and wisdom necessary in order to function in life. McLuhan characterizes this early culture as a magical world of sound, a world where persons who gave forth sounds for human ears were absolutely indispensable for human life and existence.

Most of us are aware of the power of the spoken word through our knowledge of the Hebrew people in the Old Testament. Think a moment on the story of Isaac announcing his blessing upon Jacob in Genesis 27. There is simply no way to comprehend that story without understanding that the *word* of blessing creates a blessing and the *word* of curse creates a curse. Furthermore we must understand that a word once sent forth from the mouth of the speaker could not be called back. The word, good or bad, was set loose in the world to create new realities.

When people talk about God's word they are talking about a word that corresponds to the human sense of hearing. God's word and *ears* belong together. We'll jump ahead of ourselves just a bit here in order to indicate that in our Western Civilization people have thought of God's word and *eyes* as belonging together. It makes an enormous difference in our understanding of God's word and of preaching whether we live in a culture that associates word (as in Word of God) with the sense of hearing (ear) or with the sense of seeing (eye). In fact, that is McLuhan's simple but profound distinction between early and modern cultures. Western Civilization, he says, has offered human beings an *eye for an ear*.

Early human society, the society which was the framework for the Bible's stories, was an ear-oriented society. This began to change, according to McLuhan's theory, with the development of the Greek *phonetic* alphabet. The phonetic alphabet, as opposed to other types of alphabets, began the process of separation between ear and eye. The phonetic alphabet, in McLuhan's scheme, is the crucial middle step on the way to the Gutenberg galaxy. It takes this step by creating a sensory imbalance. The phonetic alphabet was the first alphabet which basically eliminated the necessity of the sense of hearing. Many of the readers of this book will have studied Hebrew. In order to read Hebrew, especially in its pre-Masoretic form where there are no vowels, the reader must supply the sounds of the vowels (*ears* have to hear the word!) in order to decipher what is on the page. To read most ancient alphabets the reader needs at least two senses: seeing and hearing.

The Greek phonetic alphabet is different. It separates sight from sound, thought from action, eye from ear. The phonetic alphabet as you read it (indeed as you read it at this precise moment) requires only one sense: sight, the eye. The letters you are now reading mean what they "see." In and of themselves the letters have no meaning and they would need no sound. (Schools credit themselves as being successful when they have taught us to read in such a way that we do not "sound out" the words with our lips. When we learned to become solely dependent on the sense of sight [our eyes] in reading, we had achieved one of the primary goals of reading instruction.)

Another characteristic of an ear-oriented world is that people live in total interdependence and interrelationship with other living and speaking human beings. The phonetic alphabet, argues McLuhan, made it possible to move from ear to eye; to move out of the human interdependence and interrelationship associated with the auditory world.

> Only the phonetic alphabet makes a break between eye and ear, between semantic meaning and visual code; and thus only phonetic writing has the power to translate

man from the tribal to the civilized sphere, to give him an eye for an ear.[1]

Having made this simple sensory perception regarding human culture, McLuhan goes on to make a number of sweeping conclusions about the shape of the Greek world in the aftermath of the sensory shock waves created by the invention of the phonetic alphabet. Those conclusions are intriguing even if we might consider them a bit grandiose. McLuhan is convinced, for example, that the Greeks invented their art and their scientific novelties after they had adopted the phonetic alphabet. The alphabet, he argues, *linearizes* life. (Scientists have discovered pre-phonetic languages which are structurally non-linear. Attempting to read these languages gives me a good idea of how we presuppose linearity in thought!)

Let me seek to illustrate the basis for this assertion. If you are absolutely dependent on your ears for all your learning you are often taking in sounds for your learning process from all directions at once. The ear has a 360° axis for learning. Eyes, however, especially eyes following the words on a page, have a very narrow field of vision. Eyes that are reading definitely experience a linear world! Your experience as you read this book is distinctly linear. Everything is in *lines*. One letter follows the last letter; one word follows another, one page follows another.

McLuhan is convinced that the Greeks *interiorized* this linear perspective on life and began to organize their world line by line. Linearity gives rise to uniformity, continuity, logical connections and so on. Greek science, art, logic, and geometry all flow out of the "interiorization" of the phonetic alphabet. This Hellenistic phonetic interiorization has had its effect on all of western culture. The western world, according to McLuhan, has really set about the systematic linearization of human life. This process was given its greatest impetus with the invention of the printing press: the Gutenberg galaxy. Post-Gutenberg culture, a culture whose dominant sense is the eye, really seeks to have its whole world look like a book! Everything should be in order. Nothing should be out of place. Cities should be built so there is some logic to their layout. (Just think of the difference in street layout in pre-Gutenberg and post-Gutenberg cities! Which do you like the best?) Cities, classrooms, modern buildings, churches—all are built to satisfy the linear sense of sight.

The invention of the printing press, therefore, which was made possible by the creation of the phonetic alphabet about 2000 years earlier, is the most significant human achievement in moving from the medieval world to the modern world. That at least is McLuhan's argument. Civilization moved, according to McLuhan, from a stage dominated by the auditory sense (ear) to a print stage dominated by the visual sense (eye). Culture changes precisely when such sensory imbalances are created. The world we have inherited from those who have gone before us is a world dominated by print and by the sense of sight. McLuhan spells out some of the characteristics of the Gutenberg galaxial world we have inherited:

1. It is a world that puts its *accent on the individual.* Print is the technology of individualism. With print it is possible for us to learn enormous amounts of information sitting *alone* in a library with a book in our hands, eyes following line upon line.

2. Learning becomes *visual.* The world of sound becomes superflous, indeed intrusive, for the acquisition of most knowledge. Those big signs that stare at you when you enter a library say: BE QUIET.

3. *Grammar and dictionaries* became indispensable. No one ever made a grammatical mistake or misspelled a word in an ear-oriented culture! Grammar and dictionaries fix and freeze the meaning of words. We are to use words according to the rules. They can no longer be the playful words of the storytellers' art.

4. That which is *logical* is that which *is linear*. When we don't understand something we almost always make linear statements to the one who has puzzled us. "I don't *follow* you." "Where are you *going* with that idea?" "I *lost* the thread of your thought." A linear progression of thought obviously makes sense to us.

5. In order to better understand a printed text the reader requires someone to help throw *light on* that text. The assumption is that the meaning is *in* the text. If light can be shed on the text then we can understand it.

On the other hand, the pre-Gutenberg world of the Middle Ages understood handwritten manuscripts and the windows of its great cathedrals as instruments which *light* might shine *through* in order that the many layers of reality behind the medium might be exposed. *Light through* assumes that there are many layers of reality behind the text. *Light on* assumes that the reality is the text. Think of the difference that makes in approaching and interpreting the Bible! The *light on* assumption presupposes that the whole meaning of the text is contained in the frozen words on the page. The *light through* assumption presupposes that a text is a medium or vehicle through which many layers of reality can be exposed; "lit up."

6. When a text (think of the Bible!) is understood as a *light on* phenomenon then we as readers of the text are

to fix our attention on that text with a high degree of intensity. We are to have a *fixed point of view.* Our eyes are stationary objects viewing another stationary object: the text. Our goal is to learn all we can about this particular configuration of letters and words. Our goal in reading a text is to acquire information, accumulate data, amass facts, assimilate ideas, etc.

Auditory culture—the phonetic alphabet—the Gutenberg galaxy: a sensory movement from ear to eye. That has been our movement through McLuhan thus far. Before we orbit out of the Gutenberg galaxy and into the world of electric media it might be interesting to call your attention to one of McLuhan's few theological comments in relationship to the process he is describing.

> The miseries of conflict between the Eastern and the Roman churches, for example, are a merely obvious instance of the type of opposition between the oral and the visual cultures, having nothing to do with the Faith.[2]

The Medium Is the Massage

What comes after Gutenberg? What kind of a sensory world do we live in? The answer, according to McLuhan, is that we live in an electric world which massages all of our senses at once. From the telegraph, to the telephone, to the radio, to the movie, to television we have lived through a period of human culture that has electrically stimulated our entire nervous system with all of its senses.

> Media, by altering the environment, evoke in us unique ratios of sense perceptions. The extension of any one sense alters the way we think and act—the way we perceive the world. When these ratios change, men change.[3]

When the ratios in the way our senses are stimulated (massaged!) change, humanity and culture changes. A culture in which the eye is predominantly massaged is different from a culture in which the ear is predominantly massaged. A culture in which all of our senses are massaged by electric media is different from the world of Gutenberg and the eye. The medium through which we learn is just as important for understanding our life and culture as what we learn through the medium. In other words, *the medium is the massage!!* An electric massage is quite different from a print massage. To fail to understand the radically different nature of this massage upon us is to fail to understand what is happening to us in this particular hour of the world's cultural history.

McLuhan writes book upon book seeking to explain for us what is happening to us in the 20th century as a result of this electric massage of all of our senses. I am going to try to summarize his views by discussing what he means by his metaphors: *hot* and *cool.*

> A hot medium is one that extends one single sense in "high definition." High definition is the state of being well filled with data. A photograph is, visually, "high definition." A cartoon is "low definition," simply because very little visual information is provided. Telephone is a cool medium, or one of low definition, because the ear is given a meager amount of information. And speech is a cool medium of low definition, because so little is given and so much has to be filled in by the listener. On the other hand, hot media do not have so much to be filled in or completed by the audience. Hot media are, therefore, low in participation, and cool media are high in participation or completion by the audience.[4]

This distinction between "hot" and "cool" is one of the most difficult to understand and consequently most misunderstood aspects of McLuhan's work. The easiest way to try to understand what he is getting at is by thinking of hot and cool in terms of how many of our five senses are involved in a particular process of communication. The fewer the number of senses actively involved, the hotter the medium. The greater the number of senses actively involved the cooler the medium. Reading, therefore, is hot because it only involves a single sense: sight. Television, on the other hand, is cool. More of our senses participate in this communication medium. Our ears must be added to our eyes. Beyond that it is McLuhan's contention that physiologically speaking our eyes must work much harder and do many more jobs while watching TV than while reading a book. The letters on a printed page are stationary. The image on a TV screen, however, is composed of a fluid sequence of electronic dots. Our eyes have to work very actively in order to organize these dots into meaningful patterns of recognition. In a very real sense we become the TV screen. It is in our bodies that the information communicated by the TV set is organized.

There is a way of testing this hot-cool hypothesis. You may have already experienced something like it. Put on a slide show for an inter-generational group of people. Those in the audience weaned on Gutenberg (chronological age is not always an accurate barometer!) will want the slides to proceed one by one (in *linear* fashion) with ample time allowed, 15-20 seconds, for viewing each slide shown. A full explanation of each slide is expected. This is a "hot" slide show. There is time to take in all of the information in linear order. The viewer does not need to participate in the program by completing what might be left out in his or her own world of imagination. All the information needed is given.

The pace of such a showing will bore those in the audience weaned on the total massage of electric circuitry: "electric people." If, however, the slides are shown on two or more screens at 2-5 second intervals with a sound track of musical background and a sound track with brief hints or clues of what it is all about, the boredom factor will decrease. (It is absolutely incredible how much visual and auditory stimuli "electronic people" can absorb simultaneously.) As viewers they are now watching a program that is "cool." It has a very low sense of definition which demands that they actively participate (participation is a *sensate* word in this context) in the process completing in their own interior world that which has been stimulated by the outer electronic barrage (massage). At this stepped up pace, however, the complaints of the "Gutenberg" people will grow increasingly audible. "Slow it down!" they will cry.

By his use of the words *hot* and *cool,* McLuhan is trying to say that *electric media have revitalized our senses.* If it is true that the phonetic alphabet and the Gutenberg press accentuated one sense (sight) to the practical anesthetization of our other sense, then we may be able to describe the effect of electric media as a total *re-sensitization.* The eye alone cannot make it in the 20th century. (Witness the confusion when it is confronted with a *multi*-media event.)

The new media (radio, movies, television, electric music, etc.) have revitalized our senses. We live today in a highly *sensate* culture. We all know that even if we do not have complex theories for explaining the phenomenon. In this process of being re-sensitized McLuhan argues that electric-age-people have a closer experiential relationship in life to early auditory cultures than to the immediately preceding Gutenberg culture. The teenager enmeshed in his or her stereophonic world is certainly caught up in an *auditory* environment! "Gutenberg" parents plead, "Please turn that down. It hurts my *ears.*" Life should approximate a library!

Incidentally, it is a documented fact that verbal and mathematical scores (linear skills!) on the Scholastic Aptitude Test have been on the decline in the U.S. since 1963, i.e., since the rise of the first generation that grew up with television. Most observers of this reality mention the possibility that McLuhan's observations on culture and senses may help explain this phenomena. A *cooled* off generation appears to have difficulty with *hot* skills!

Some McLuhanesque Soundings in Theology

We have traced in a very broad way Marshall McLuhan's approach to understanding human culture. I wish now to indicate some of the theological realities that I began to see in a new way as a result of this journey through the McLuhan maze. They will lead us very quickly into our primary subject: preaching.

1. *Verbal Inspiration and Propositional Revelation are theories very much at home in the Gutenberg world of thought.*

The idea that the biblical authors and manuscripts were verbally inspired is an ancient view in the church. Complete trust in the inspired words meaning the words on a *printed* page, however, was not possible until the advent of the Gutenberg press. In the post-Gutenberg world talk about the Bible as the *word* of God was oftentimes *eye* talk. The word of God was what one could see with one's eyes when the Bible was read. When "Word of God" talk becomes "book-talk" then the Bible is read and understood from a *fixed point of view* and its readers seek to have *light on* the text in order to understand the information and ideas that the text teaches.

A comparatively recent quotation from a conservative

Lutheran journal underscores very heavily this sense that the Bible is a book for eyes. Biblical inspiration has to do with authorship and information. The inspiration of Scripture is understood to mean,

> . . . the information contained in this Holy Bible was made known to the human writers whom God selected in such a way that their finished product was exactly what God wanted written. This feature of inspiration protected the *message that God wanted to transmit* so that it would not be altered or affected by those who were his instruments in its presentation. In three areas of happening God revealed basic and pertinent *information* to and through his messengers: what for them was past, current, future. . . . In His wisdom and providence, God had a way for that *essential information* to be delivered and preserved . . . IN and THROUGH A WRITTEN RECORD.[5]

Read that quotation again. Can you imagine what that paragraph could have meant to a person living in an auditory culture? Could it really have any meaning to people in a pre-Gutenberg culture? It's doubtful. This view of Scripture appears to be a view totally dominated by the impact of the Gutenberg galaxy.

Propositional revelation, a way of understanding God's revelation to human beings, is an understanding of revelation that is very much at home in the Gutenberg area. It is a highly logical counterpart to the view of verbal inspiration which we have just discovered. Propositional revelation is a view of revelation which understands God's revelation to have taken the form of propositional statements as found on the printed page of the Bible. The Bible, therefore, is a collection of true and correct propositions and statements about God. Witness the following quotation:

> The Christian doctrine is not produced by the theologian; all that the Christian theologian does is that he compiles

> the doctrinal statements contained in Scripture. . . .
> Theology is not made up of the variable notions and
> opinions of men, but is the immutable divine truth or
> God's own doctrine.[6]

What is revelation? It is hot. It is linear. It is what your eyes read in a book. It is information. It is a collection of truths. In other words, all that we have to say about revelation corresponds to the cultural world created by the Gutenberg galaxy. Again we can ask: "What would a person living in an auditory culture make out of such an understanding of revelation?" It is a statement which comes out of a period of human culture when printed words and eyes were the dominant massage.

2. *The task of preaching under the cultural impact of the Gutenberg press is necessarily hot, linear, and didactic.*

There are certainly a variety of streams that have converged to produce the didactic type of preaching. The cultural movement which we call the Enlightenment with its emphasis on reason, order, logic, and science has had its impact on the "science" of preaching. New studies in human consciousness talk of the left-hemisphere of the brain as that part of our brain that is

> . . . predominantly involved with analytic, logical thinking, especially in verbal and mathematical functions. Its mode of operation is primarily linear. This hemisphere seems to process information sequentially. This mode of operation of necessity must underlie logical thought. . . . [7]

Perhaps preaching has come under the dominance of the left hemisphere of the brain!

It is not possible to track down all the factors that have produced didactic preaching. To the extent that the Gutenberg galaxy has dominated the world of preaching it is possible to point to the absolute logic of its development.

As print became the dominant sensory massage, the Word of God was understood increasingly as a printed book to which we relate primarily through the sense of sight. Revelation is subsequently understood as that which is printed in the book for our eyes to read and for our minds to comprehend. Preaching becomes the task of translating eye information (that which is in the book) into ear information. Preaching becomes the task of passing along the true and essential *doctrines* and *information* of God's Word to the listening audience. Preaching becomes didactic!

The sense of sight, the eye, could give us a definition of the Word of God (it is a verbally inspired book), a definition of revelation (propositional) and an understanding of the basic Christian task of pulpit communication (didactic). What do all these definitions mean if it is true that we now live in a period of cultural transition wherein the Gutenberg massage of the eye is giving way to an electric massage of our entire sensory being? Does that mean that all of our "Gutenberg definitions" are in need of a massage?

3. *Hot liturgy bores cool people.*

Most Protestant liturgy is very hot! (This is increasingly true of Roman Catholic liturgical experience.) A hot liturgical and worship life is characterized by many of the following Gutenberg phenomena. It is linear and orderly in character. Everything has its rightful place. We follow the *order* of service. It is characterized by high definition and low participation. The high definition character of worship is best illustrated by making reference to the enormous amount of data that is imparted. Lessons are read, hymn verses sung, prayers prayed, sermons preached—the amount of data we are asked to consume is seemingly endless. Most of our churches are still linear in design. We sit in our pews as disconnected from other people as any of the letters on this page are disconnected from each other.

I have heard a number of people who have not grown up in this hot, didactic, linear order of worship complain that it bores them. I think we need to be very careful about how we hear such a complaint. It is not a complaint about the *message;* it is a complaint about the *massage!*

Electric people, people whose senses have been revitalized by radio, television, movies, etc., find this worship world, dominated by the visual sense, to be a very slow moving world. It is a sensory experience that is out of step with their normal experience of life. Electric people will probably always be bored by Gutenberg orders of worship. A concomitant reality, and one that most concerns us, is that electric people are generally bored by Gutenberg (i.e., didactic) *preaching* as well!

Characteristics of Didactic Preaching

How we understand and interpret Scripture predisposes how we understand the task of preaching. To put that in more sophisticated theological language: *hermeneutics predisposes homiletics.* In the preceding pages we have sketched the outlines of a Gutenberg hermeneutic. Gutenberg hermeneutics, dominated by the visual sense, understands the Word of God to be that which is on the printed page. God's revelation is God's way of getting the truths that he wants to teach humanity on that page for us to have, hold, and learn from. Gutenberg hermeneutics, therefore, understands the Bible to be the perfect deposit of all of God's truths. *Gutenberg hermeneutics predis-*

poses a didactic form of homiletics. Gutenberg homiletics
would have the following characteristics:

- the goal of preaching is to teach the lessons of the text.
- in order to teach the lessons or meaning of the text the
points to be made are usually abstracted from the text.
- the sermon is aimed primarily at the hearer's mind.
- the sermon is developed in a logical, sequential and
linear manner.
- the sermon is prepared under the criteria for written
material.
- the faith engendered in the hearer is "faith" that the
ideas are true.

We will discuss these characteristics in the pages that
follow. It is important to note, however, that up until this
point I have been following a *theoretical* path of investigation. I have made generalized theological deductions
from McLuhan's theories. We have talked theoretically
about a Gutenberg hermeneutic. Gutenberg hermeneutics
presuppose a theoretical type of homiletics—namely, Gutenberg homiletics. Gutenberg homiletics has several characteristics—and these are *precisely the characteristics
that dominate homiletical practice in our time.* My theoretical homiletic, derived from the Gutenberg Galaxy, is,
in actual practice, the homiletical style (the didactic sermon) which is practiced by the preachers of our time.

McLuhan's theories have helped me isolate some issues
concerning preaching. Thinking within his framework I
have seen some hermeneutical/homiletical interrelation-
ships that I had not seen before. Having seen these inter-
relationships from a new perspective I believe that I have
gained some helpful insights into the dynamics of "didactic" preaching; the dominant preaching typology of our
time. I am not arguing that there is a kind of inevitable
link between human cultural transition in the way that

McLuhan perceives it and homiletical practice. Not at all! I would assume that we have arrived at our current didactic homiletical practice through any number of avenues. The ability to describe those avenues lies beyond my present knowledge.

What I would like to maintain is that didactic preaching dominates the present homiletical world and that what typifies that world is a set of characteristics which *parallels* the characteristics I have advanced for Gutenberg homiletics. Didactic preaching is not necessarily a result of the cultural phenomena described by McLuhan. It was in reading and thinking through the theories of McLuhan, however, that I came to see the shape, possibilities and problems of didactic preaching for the first time.

1. *The goal of preaching is to teach the lessons of the text.*

In other words, didactic preaching has points to make, data to impart, information to communicate. The sermon is an attempt to throw *light on* the *meaning* of the text, to communicate the truths of the text in such a way that the hearer believes them to be true.

Didactic preaching can be characterized as preaching that emphasizes the word "about." It is preaching *about* God's love, *about* forgiveness, *about* healing, *about* God's promises. Consider the story of the young couple who knew all about love. Whenever they met, which was as often as possible, each brought a new book from the public library on the subject of love. As they parked on lover's lane they engaged themselves in a quite different pasttime than the other young lovers. They read their books to each other. They wanted to know all *about* love. Finally, they achieved their goal. They became experts on the concept of love! A far-fetched story? Certainly. But is it any further fetched than preaching which seeks to make its hearers experts in the truth about *God's* love?

When "teaching the lessons of the text" is understood to be the central focus of the preaching task the question-answer format is often used. Some preachers and some sermons rely exclusively on the question-answer technique. The technique is a simple one. A question is asked. The question is answered. The answer leads, in turn, to another question which leads to another answer which leads to another question and so on. This is a highly developed *linear* technique which might be appropriate on paper where our *eyes* can follow the argument. The *ears* which we must rely on in listening to sermons, however, don't follow linearity all that well. (Ears can follow stories about people longer than they can follow ideas!) Ears get lost where eyes are quick to follow.

The question-answer format often has another problem. The questions are too much the questions that the preacher is asking. They do not reflect the questions the listener might ask.

Criticism of "teaching the lessons of the text" as the primary goal of preaching should not be understood as a criticism of the teaching office in the church's life. I am not against teaching! I am a teacher after all! Both preaching and teaching have their legitimate role to play in the life of the church. Preaching *proclaims* and *announces* the gospel. (See the discussion in Chapter 3.) Teaching *explains* and *clarifies* the meaning of a biblical text.

In most Sunday worship services there is a time set aside for the reading of the Bible. It might be a very helpful and useful practice to take 5-10 minutes at the time that the Bible texts are read to teach the congregation something of the background of these texts, their biblical context, the aim and goal of the writer etc. There are many things we explore in our study when we work on the sermon that have no place in the pulpit on Sunday morning. "We are to leave our scholarly research behind." I agree that the sermon is no place to drag out such research. There are a lot of "scholarly facts" about the texts we read on Sunday morning, however, that lay people ought to be informed of. Most pastors have no other opportunities to lead the assembled congregation in serious Bible study. Why not use some time for such study each Sunday when the texts are read? Furthermore, to simply "leave our research in the study" promotes a view of the laity that ought to be rejected!

It should be clear that the time taken for teaching the reading of the lessons would have to be carved out of "sermon time." Ten minutes of teaching and ten minutes of preaching (or some such appropriate balance) separated by other elements of the worship service is about all that a "cool" generation can bear!

2. *In order to teach the lessons or meaning of the text the points to be made are usually abstracted from the text.*

The type of exegetical method that abstracts points from the text that should be taught works for those texts whose primary purpose is didactic. There are not many texts which are *primarily* didactic in nature, however. This style of biblical exegesis tends to use the biblical text as a *pre-text*. What becomes important to the preacher is not the total configuration of the text as parable or miracle story or recitation of God's saving deeds. The important thing is the *meaning* of the miracle. The meaning of the miracle event is thus abstracted from the text and the sermon is a didactic sermon on the abstracted meaning. The point or meaning of John 9 (a blind man receives his sight) is *about* the opening of our eyes that we might seé God. The sermon proceeds to develop this point in various and sundry ways leaving the particular miracle of this text far behind. The text has been used as a jumping off point, as a pretext, for teaching about seeing. This is a familiar characteristic of didactic preaching.

3. *The sermon is aimed primarily at the hearer's mind.*

Using McLuhan's language we could say that didactic preaching is hot. It is high in definition (the information is carefully packaged) and low in audience participation. The hearers are called upon to *understand what has been said.* They don't need to use their imagination or any other faculty in order to complete the sermon. Everything they ought to know is laid out for them. Fully conscious, alert minds will get the point.

Homiletics professors often give reports on student preachers that verify this point. When students are asked, "What is the goal of this sermon?" they inevitably use cognitive words in their reply. "My goal is to *show.* ..." "My aim is to *teach.* ..." "I hope to *convince* them. ..." "I would really like to *persuade* them. ..." "I hope they will *understand.* ..." If these are the only kinds of words that we can come up with to designate the aim or goal of our preaching then it is quite clear that we predominantly understand preaching as a mental exercise.

Henry Mitchell has written a book entitled, *The Recovery of Preaching.* Mitchell is a black Baptist preacher and teacher of preaching. The book is an analysis of black preaching for what it may have to contribute to the American pulpit at large. Mitchell makes a crucial point of what he calls the "target of black preaching."

> "To what *aspect* of all these persons do we preach? To what process(es) of personality is the gospel directed?"

> . . . Black preaching assumes a target of whole persons. The largely cerebral appeal of most White preaching would seem to imply a primarily intellectual target, with the homiletic skills sought and taught focusing on the production of a stimulating idea. In contrast to this I see in the African-American continuum of religious experience and practice an answer that lies in the *combination* of the intellectual with the less rational but equally valid processes, . . . the best of the Black preaching tradition has synthesized the appeal to the conscious and the so-called unconscious with a unique clarity and intensity.[8]

Mitchell contends that the difference between black preaching and white preaching is that black preaching is anchored in an oral culture.

> . . . today's technical developments in mass media have helped us to go back to the oral in even such print-oriented fields as public education. The process has come full circle, and the style of Black oral communication is the wave not only of the past but of the future.[9]

Shades of Marshall McLuhan! Mitchell's book is extremely provocative in setting forth the characteristics of black/oral preaching which is "transconscious" in its effect. "Transconscious" is a word used to include the conscious and subconscious aspects of human personality. Mitchell's book is well worth reading.

With Mitchell's words in front of us we now have an alternative answer to the question concerning the aim or goal of preaching. Preaching would not have to be conceived of solely in terms of reaching the *mind* of the hearer. Transconscious possibilities do exist!

The necessity of developing aims for preaching that go beyond the mind (point-making, lesson-teaching, information-passing) has occurred to me most vividly in my own experience. I indicated in the preface that I listen to a lot of sermons. I do not come to those sermons as a *tab-*

ula rasa, a blank page. Sometimes I take my seat in the pew aglow and alive with joy of the Christian faith. Any human problems seem quite far removed from my world. On those days any sermon will do!

At other times, however, I take my seat burdened with the variety of human hurts, pains and anxieties that plague us all from time to time. It is on those days, especially on those days, that I find myself simply passed by in the typically didactic sermon. Ideas, lessons or points aimed at my mind simply do not reach me where I live. My children have caused me moments of despair. My job overwhelms and crushes me. My heart aches for the poor of this world. All the ideas, lessons and points in the world simply do not offer balm for such wounds. That, for me, is the final poverty of didactic preaching. It too often sends me home with three nice points but with no word of healing for my broken heart.

4. *The sermon is developed in a logical, sequential, linear manner.* As we have tried to understand the theses of Marshall McLuhan, this fact of life about sermon development could certainly have roots in the Gutenberg penchant for satisfying the sense of the eye (order, balance, etc.) It may go back even further into Greek phonetic culture. Early Hellenistic rules for rhetoric were certainly characterized by logic, sequence and linearity. Most textbooks on homiletics are forthright in admitting that much of what has become the wisdom of the Christian community about preaching has its roots in the Greek rhetorical tradition.

It has become a common bit of humor in many Christian traditions to talk about the "three point" sermon. This assumes that all sermons should have three points and that when a sermon is an exception to that rule some kind of explanation is necessary. There is certainly nothing wrong with a three-point sermon or with a three-point development which is logical and linear in nature. Many homiletics textbooks spend a good deal of time instructing us in the art of arranging our three points. They should come in order of ascending importance, be of approximately equal length, etc.

I think the problem lies in the fact that this three-point, sequential format has become a straight-jacket. How else could a sermon be constructed? Is there any other way? I suspect that for many preachers putting a sermon together is a weekly matter of *rearranging* a biblical text so that it fits into a prefabricated, three-point mold. To the extent that that is true for us our sermon preparation owes far more of its shape to Greek rhetoric and Gutenberg linearity than it does to the particular literary form of the biblical text that is before us. Why should preaching be primarily conceived of by anyone as the task of taking biblical material that has its own unique life and forms and casting it into a form that has been borrowed from an altogether different culture?

The first major problem with logical, sequential, linear sermons is that in most cases such a format imposes an alien format on the particular literary form of the biblical text which lies before us. Not many biblical texts are constructed in point-by-point, linear fashion. Many portions of Paul's letters would come close to such a form. Almost all of the Old Testament and most of the material in the gospels, however, comes to us in a variety of literary forms none of which is crafted in points, linearity, logic or sequence.

A second major problem in the emphasis on linear development is that *linearity is primarily a medium for eyes*. Linearity is for eyes, not necessarily for ears.

Preaching, however, is for ears and not for eyes. Some preachers seek to overcome this gap by printing the *outline* of their sermon in the bulletin. As preachers our eyes are meant to be directed at the eyes of our hearers, not at our notes. The words that count are not the words as they appear to us on our nicely typed sermon notes but the words the congregation hears with their ears. What we *see* (our sermon notes) and what they *hear* can be two different things. Ears, as McLuhan reminds us, have a 360° field of "vision." Ears are not instruments of linearity! Ears get bored rather easily by linearity and when ears get bored, minds wander!

The *outlines* for most sermons on a text concerning a miracle performed by Jesus and the outline of a class lesson on miracles would not, in most cases, differ significantly. Our understanding of preaching and our understanding of teaching (didactic) are often nearly indistinguishable.

5. *The sermon is prepared under the criteria for written material.* The reasons for this are very similar to those presented above. A simple word of caution is in order. *Sermons are to be heard, not read.* They should, therefore, be prepared under criteria for oral communication rather than under criteria for print communication. They should be prepared for ears, not eyes.

The church is still very much a creature of the oral culture. But the communication skills most of us have learned have more to do with writing and reading than with speaking and hearing. Most of us have lost the ability to compose for the oral occasion. The quality of sermons steadily declines because our preachers read rather than proclaim the Word. What they say is so governed by the prose of print that most listeners cannot grasp the thought. . . . The language of print is much more concerned with meaning than with sound as it should be. . . . Our pastors especially should learn the effective use of images and stories, techniques from the oral culture which can make their sermons more memorable and more compelling.[10]

Clyde Fant, in his book, *Preaching for Today,* makes the same point in a chapter entitled, "Out of the Gutenberg Galaxy." He discusses the nineteenth century as a great age of literature. During that age preaching followed a literate culture and became more literate and less oral in its character. The problem that Fant sees is that the great *literary preachers* of the nineteenth century increasingly became, and remain for the twentieth century student, the models of effective preaching and communication. Fant sees this movement as a movement toward guaranteed obsolescence for preaching.

In making his point he reminds us of another of McLuhan's dictums about culture: *the lively communication medium for one generation becomes the art form for the next generation.* This McLuhanesque dictum can be illustrated with a reference to radio. Quite often when I am driving in my car with my radio on I will happen to catch a station that is airing old programs from radio's heyday in the '30s and '40s. Usually the host(s) of the program will help explain the original context of the programs be it Amos 'n Andy, Jack Benny, Fred Allen, Lum 'n Abner or the Lone Ranger. These programs were yesterday's lively forms of communication; today they are an art form.

Fant is afraid that if preaching today is modeled on the literary preaching style of the nineteenth century it will simply become an art form; it will not be a lively, effective, contemporary form of communication. Any good results which might come from this process of learning how to preach are outweighed in Fant's mind by one great problem:

Students were encouraged, directly or indirectly, to *write* sermons like the ones they were reading. As a result, the sermon was increasingly prepared for the eye rather than the ear. Devices suited for reading—paragraphing, formal syntax, tightly fitted logical arguments, complex outlines, literary language—were superimposed upon the sermon. Of course the sermon continued to be delivered orally, but increasingly from a manuscript really prepared for reading. Like a satellite trapped within the gravitational pull of a planet, preaching has been locked into the Gutenberg galaxy. The sermon must break out of this orbit if it is to be able to communicate within its own medium.[11]

Mitchell's book, *The Recovery of Preaching*, argues that it is precisely at this point that white-print-culture can learn something from black preaching which is preaching born out of an oral culture and tradition.

The oral processes, long lost in most Western societies because of the advent of the printing press, have survived amazingly well in such places as West Africa. And the Black Church in America has been built not on the literacy denied slaves and their descendants, but on the African cultural bias for massive memory, lively renditions/"readings" and supportive situational sharing, whether in ceremony or simple conversation. The early biblical method of verbally passing on the history/gospel is alive and well today, mostly unidentified as such among the very people who practice it best.[12]

Didactic preaching is often characterized by the fact that it is prepared for the eye, prepared to be read, rather than being prepared to be heard. When we prepare something that is to be read our concern is with proper grammatical style, good syntax, proper paragraphing, etc. When we prepare something to be heard, something for the ear, then we have to think about rhythm, pacing, repetition (think of how jokes rely on repetition and suspense!), mnemonic devices, active verbs, etc. We must constantly ask ourselves, "How will this sound?" Most black preachers and most southern preachers are good models to emulate in striving for good oral communication. When Martin Luther King rhythmically and repeatedly intoned, "I have a dream . . ." we remember! Even white-folks start to say "Amen." That's oral communication!

Next time Billy Graham's crusade is on television *listen* to his preaching. Listen to his oral style! He may have a sentence ten lines long on paper but he never dishes out more than about ten words at a time for your ear to latch on to. There lies a good clue to oral style. *Watch out for long sentences.* Sometime ago I began to ask myself why I was bored by certain sermons. Then I discovered "Jensen's First Law of a Boring Sermon." I simply ask myself, "How long are the sentences?" Invariably that is the only question I have to ask to explain my disinterest. The sentences are simply too long for my ears to follow. They would read well; they sound terrible. Try the "Law" out the next time you find yourself bored with a sermon. Watch the length of sentences in your own preaching. Write out what you want heard, not what you want read.

I don't know all the secrets of oral communication. But I think I know a few of them. Beyond that I would urge you to pay attention to good models and to read some of the experts in the field to discover for yourself other secrets of good oral communication. Let's say that a sermon has in it this simple statement: "Jesus is our Savior and our Redeemer and our Lord." As you read this sentence on this printed page your eyes automatically pick out the words that are important: Savior, Redeemer, Lord. Now try to imagine yourself actually hearing that sentence. It is a real earful! In fact, it's too much for most ears to take in one brief, fast moving sentence. For the

ears of the listener that simple sentence needs to be recast. It will look funny to you as I rewrite it for preaching
but if you can imagine yourself hearing it you will get
the point. In a sermon it might be said this way:

Jesus is our *Savior* (pause); Jesus is our *Redeemer*
(another pause for the ear); Jesus is our *Lord*. That
reads funny; it sounds good. (The italics indicate which
words would be orally accented.)

I have mentioned repetition as a key to good oral communication. (Ears can't go back and re-read a sentence.)
Most of us have heard the advice supposedly given by a
backwoods preacher: "First I tells 'em what I is going to
tell 'em; then I tells 'em; then I tells 'em what I told
'em." That's good advice!

In my church's tradition it is customary to have young
people in confirmation classes hand in sermon outlines.
(That's one way to make them listen!) There is a sense
in which this assignment of an outline *presupposes* that
the sermon is created under the canons of written material. It might be better to ask them to write down what
happened to them in the sermon. A question like, "What
did you *experience* in the sermon?" immediately moves
the thinking of both preacher and listener to an *oral*
rather than a *literary* concept of the sermon.

I agree with Henry Mitchell when he suggests that the
sermon has "transconscious" possibilities. Sermons ought
to reach the conscious mind and the subconscious being.
Sermons ought to reach minds and hearts and thoughts
and emotions. To reach the "transconscious" realms of the
listener many of the primal instincts of oral communication are absolutely essential.

It is a tragedy that so many fine sermons are presented
in such a flat, prosaic, logical, rational, "hot" manner
that they do not stir the listener. As preachers we ought to

have greater respect than that for our hearers. Preaching is oral communication. Oral communication (oratory!) is an art most of us would do well to practice and perfect. Our audience and the oral character of the gospel itself demand that of us!

6. *The faith engendered in the hearer is faith that the ideas presented are true.* All preaching aspires to create and strengthen faith in the life of the hearer. Christian traditions are divided according to how they understand faith. The classic debate on the subject is usually about where faith begins. Some argue that faith is *generated by the hearer* in response to the story of Jesus. Others argue that faith is *generated by God;* only God through the instrument of the Holy Spirit can create faith in the hearer. Christians find themselves in a state of honest disagreement on this issue.

Earlier I contended that the doctrine of the verbal inspiration of Scripture, the understanding of revelation as propositional in nature and a view of preaching that is didactic in character are companion ideas all of which may be understood in relation to the Gutenberg galaxy. These companion ideas present us with their own understanding of faith. In this context, faith is that Christian response which believes that the propositions in Scripture which are verbally inspired are true. Didactic preaching presents us with the correct biblical ideas and doctrines. A faithful response to didactic preaching is to believe that what has been said is true. Being a *true* Christian means believing the *right* (i.e. orthodox) things.

This relatively recent understanding of faith can easily be discerned as a major cause of the sharp differences between denominations. Denominations arise because different denominations believe different doctrines to be true.

The "faithful" ones in every denomination (faith understood as believing the right things) are always out to purge from their midst those who do not believe the right things. This unbiblical (where in Scripture is faith understood in this radically cognitive way?) understanding of faith has been the cause for many scandalous Christian schisms.

In the Bible faith has to do with a trust relationship between persons. The followers of Jesus were those who trusted him, his mission and his promises. Faith is trust in the word Jesus is and utters. Jesus, God's-word-made-flesh, shapes our life and destiny. Our faith (or trust) is engendered by the power of Jesus' word as it enters our life. Faith is life lived out of the graciousness of Jesus' word to us. However, where faith gets turned around somehow to mean "believing the right ideas and doctrines *about* (there's that word again) Jesus," then faith becomes a cognitive, mental, rational *good work*. Didactic preaching which presents the true doctrines about Jesus for people to have faith in can, therefore, be preaching that leads people to life under a new law: If you wish to be a Christian *you must believe* the right doctrines. The gracious word of Jesus which invites and evokes faith gets turned into just another legalistic system.

Afterword

Reuel Howe compiled six complaints that laypeople raised with him over and over about the nature and character of the preaching they heard. When I read the list I was struck by how many of these complaints would fit the criticisms I have made in this chapter of didactic preaching. Howe's list is as follows:

(1) sermons often contain too many complex ideas;

(2) sermons have too much analysis and too little answer;

(3) sermons are too formal and too impersonal;

(4) sermons use too much theological jargon;

(5) sermons are too propositional; not enough illustrations;

(6) too many sermons simply reach a dead end and give no guidance to commitment and action.[13]

Armed with material like this quotation from Reuel Howe and convinced by a number of factors of the deficiency of didactic preaching, I have been sharply critical of a kind of preaching that is probably used by most preachers on most Sunday mornings. I may have been too critical. There are many texts of Scripture which could be treated didactically. Didactic methods of presenting a text are available that would avoid most of the criticisms I have presented. There are positive aspects of didactic preaching I have not discussed.

Why have I not discussed the positive aspects? Why has my treatment of didactic preaching not been more even-handed? I hope the rest of the book will speak to these questions. I am deeply concerned by what I perceive to be the almost total dominance in the American pulpit of a preaching style that is closely akin to didactic preaching. It is a kind of preaching that has its own merits but which is also woefully inadequate to carry the whole load of preaching.

I hope you will think seriously about my reservations cited to this dominance of didactic preaching. I am convinced that if we think about these matters together we may develop ways to preach the gospel that are more effective for our time. My intention has been to enlist you in the process of thinking about preaching; not to discredit what you have been doing! If, however, you find yourself in a didactic preaching rut, you may have needed the pointed character of my remarks to jog you into that thinking process.

Notes

1. Marshall McLuhan, *The Gutenberg Galaxy* (New York: Signet, 1969) 38.
2. Ibid., 86.
3. Marshall McLuhan and Quentin Fiore, *The Medium Is the Massage* (New York: Bantam, 1967) 41.
4. Marshall McLuhan, *Understanding Media: The Extensions of Man* (New York: Signet, 1964) 36.
5. *The Word Alone*, July, 1964. Italics mine.
6. Francis Pieper, *Christian Dogmatics* (St. Louis: Concordia, 1950) 51-52.
7. Robert E. Ornstein, *The Psychology of Consciousness* (New York: Viking, 1972) 51-52.
8. Henry H. Mitchell, *The Recovery of Preaching* (San Francisco: Harper & Row, 1977) 12-13.
9. Ibid., 24.
10. Gracia Grindal, "Stopping by the Pit Stop," *The Christian Century,* May 11, 1977, 454-455.
11. Clyde Fant, *Preaching for Today* (New York: Harper & Row, 1975) 112-113.
12. Mitchell, 75.
13. Quoted in Fant, 8.

2

A DIDACTIC SERMON

I indicated in the introduction that following the chapters that describe the various preaching types there would follow a sermon (s) illustrating the type that has been described. This chapter, therefore, consists solely of one sermon on Luke 15:11-32. I have chosen this text because I feel that without violating the character of the text it can be used as the text for three different sermons in this book each illustrating a different type. At the close of each chapter describing sermon types, therefore, there will be a sermon on this same text. I hope in this way you will be able to discern clearly the differences in preaching types that I am attempting to set forth.

A Father's Welcome

Introduction

We have all had the experience of sitting around with a group of people telling stories and jokes. As each new story is told the laughter seems to increase. As soon as one story is told and the laughter subsides there is a heightened sense of anticipation as all eagerly await the next story. Someone says, "Have you heard the one about the monkey and the tiger choosing up sides to play football in order to break the boredom of life on Noah's ark?" If the story is not familiar then the person who has asked about this particular story goes ahead and tells the joke. If, however, the question is met by a mass nodding of heads (meaning the story is well known) then the story is not told and someone else inquires, "Have you heard the one about . . . ?" In such a setting stories familiar to the audience are not retold.

Things are different than that in church. I don't have to ask you, "Have you heard the one about the prodigal son?" I don't have to ask that question because I know the answer. Of course you know the story about the prodigal son. It is a familiar story to all of you. Familiar or not, it is the text for today and I am going to proceed to read it and to preach on it.

The problem with familiar stories, of course, and that includes the prodigal son story, is that we think we know them so well that we have nothing more to learn from them. That is never the case with biblical stories. We never really exhaust their meaning no matter how often we tell and retell them. Let us examine this familiar story together again today to see what new meanings it might unfold for us.

I. We All Run from the "Heavenly" Father

A. Each of Us Has a Far Country

The story begins with a demand placed upon a father by the younger of his two sons. This son wanted his father to give him the full inheritance to which he was entitled. He wanted that inheritance in order that he might leave home and start up his own life in some faraway place.

How reminiscent this story is of the story of Adam and Eve as it is told in the third chapter of Genesis! Humanity's primal temptation has not seemed to change much through the generations. That temptation is to take what is coming to us *and more* and to strike out and live our own kind of life. Adam and Eve could not resist the temptation afforded by the fruit of the tree in the midst of the garden. If they ate of the fruit of this tree they would "be like God" promised the tempter. There we have a basic working definition of what sin is. Sin is the human temptation followed by the action of seeking to play God, to take what is ours and more and live a life centered on our own dreams, wishes and desires rather than a life centered on the heavenly Father's goals and plans for our life.

When Adam and Eve chose to sin by taking their rightful and unrightful inheritance, God punished them by banning them from the garden and casting them out into the far country. Adam and Eve wound up in a far country, the prodigal son wound up in a far country and we wind up in a far country when we choose to be the gods of our own lives. Our individual "far countries" may take the form of broken families, broken marriages, broken lives or broken hearts. When we take our lives into our own hands and seek to be our own god, we, along with Adam, Eve, the prodigal and all the rest of humanity always wind up in some far country.

B. Our Life in the Far Country Usually Ends
   in Despair

The prodigal son squandered his inheritance in the far country. After having spent all that he had he wound up feeding the pigs for one of the citizens of the far country. For the Jews the pig was considered to be an unclean animal. Therefore, when we hear that the prodigal was working among the pigs we realize that Jesus is picturing the prodigal's forsaken condition in language that those who heard the original parable immediately understood. In fact, so forsaken was his condition that the only food he had to eat was that which he shared with the swine! Given these conditions it is no wonder that the prodigal son came to his senses and realized that he lived in a pigpen called despair.

I think the meaning of this part of the story is told clearly enough so that all of us understand it. Jesus is picturing life in the far country, life that we have taken into our own hands, life apart from God, as a life that finally ends in despair. Such life must of necessity run into despair because none of us has the strength to sustain any kind of meaningful life out of our own power. When we are left alone in a far country to produce our own meaning to life we can manage only so long before despair sets in. Death, of course, is the final hurdle. We might conquer out of our power every other obstacle that stands between us and our goal of producing the kind of life we want to live. No sooner, however, are we congratulating ourselves on our fine achievement and we find ourselves facing the final obstacle: death. None of us has the power to overcome that final obstacle. Death means that our journey to the far country, our journey away from God living life the way we want to live, finally ends in despair for us all.

II. Repentance Is the Language of Return

A. How Can We Return to God?

The prodigal son finally "came to himself," as the text puts it, and realized that his situation in life was desperate and fraught with despair. When he thought back on life at home he realized that even his father's hired servants had a better life than he had. Soon the prodigal wanted to go back to his father's house in the worst possible way. But how could he do that? What would he say to his father and what would his father say to him?

The prodigal son had asked a very good question. How do we prodigals return to our heavenly Father? Within the Christian community we acknowledge that we are all sinful human beings. We have all run away from our heavenly Father. The character of that running away from God differs with each of us. We differ from each other in the ways we figure out to run away; we are like each other in that we have all run, and we continue to run away from God.

Today we find ourselves gathered together to worship God. I assume that our collective presence here today means that we have all decided that it is time to return from our runnings and wanderings. We are present here this morning and we acknowledge that God is also here. What should we say to him? How do prodigal people talk to God?

B. We Return to God Speaking the Language of Repentance

If we take the prodigal son as our model we see that he decided simply to tell his father the truth about his life. He decided to tell his father that he had sinned against him and against heaven. We call telling God the truth about our self-centered ways of life repentance. The prodigal son, therefore, decided to practice repentance.

There are many aspects of the life of the Christian community that must be a puzzle to all who observe us from a distance. It is a general rule of life that in order to be a member of any organization or of any religious community we must be able to do something to earn and keep that membership. And yet, in spite of this common rule of life, nearly every time Christians gather together to worship God they begin that time with a period of confession of sin. As we repent, we confess to God that we really don't deserve to be present in his house. Repentance, confession of sin, telling God the truth about our lives—that is how prodigal people talk when they return to God after their daily wanderings in the far country.

It is often stated that Christianity is an *offensive* religion. One of the major reasons that Christianity offends people lies in the Christian understanding of human nature as a sinful nature. As Christians we understand that we never come to God on a kind of equal footing with him; the dialog between us and God is never a dialog between equals. The dialog between human beings, prodigal people, and God is a dialog between people who have failed God and a God who listens to failing people. When we as Christians talk to God, therefore, we often begin such talk by acknowledging that we sinful people have found nothing but despair in a life that is shaped and ordered by our own designs. Our conversations with God, therefore, are nearly always conversations that begin with the language of confession. One of the chief lessons for us out of the parable of the prodigal son is that our talk when we return to God is repentance talk.

III. The Basic Character of the "Heavenly" Father Is Forgiveness

A. He Has Been Waiting for Us All the Time

After having examined carefully the plot of this story we are prepared for its central and most climactic moment. The prodigal son began his journey back home in fear and trembling at what his father might say to him. We can imagine that throughout his entire journey home the son wondered what it was that might happen to him and that while he journeyed he practiced his "coming home" speech over and over again. His coming home speech, of course, was his truth-telling moment of repentance: "Father, I have sinned against heaven and before you . . ." But how, he must have wondered, would his father respond?

The question about the response of the prodigal's father to his repenting son's return is of more than merely academic interest to us. We have understood from this story that in our own way we, too, are prodigals who have run to a far country and we desperately wish to return to God with the truth-telling language of repentance on our lips. How will this heavenly Father respond to us? The question that haunted the mind of the prodigal son as he returned home is surely the same question that haunts our minds as we seek to return to God today and every day of our lives.

For all who ask the question about the nature of the heavenly Father's response to returning prodigals this story offers a surprise which is the fundamental surprise of the gospel itself. In our natural mode of human expectations we would expect to hear and read that the prodigal's father drove a hard bargain upon the return of the prodigal. The fact of the matter is that the prodigal's father had evidently been watching daily for some sign of his son and when he saw him at a far distance down the road he went racing out of the house and down the road in order to give his son an enthusiastic welcome home embrace. The prodigal never even got a chance to deliver his well-rehearsed repentance speech! It ought to be very clear to us from this story that the prodigal was received at home not because of anything he had done and certainly not because of the effectiveness of his well-thought-out and well-rehearsed repentance speech. The son was welcomed home in grand fashion for one reason and for one reason only: his gracious and forgiving father had been waiting on tiptoes of anticipation for this day of welcome return!

B. The Biblical God Is a Forgiving God

The Christian faith, which all of us celebrate by our presence here this morning, is built primarily around the fact that in Jesus Christ we see and understand that the God of this whole universe is a God whose welcome mat is always out for prodigal people. We discover again in this story that the God and Father of our Lord Jesus Christ is a waiting and forgiving Father. That fact is a very important fact for all of us prodigals to remember and for all of us to try to comprehend.

We prodigal people are usually quite adept at understanding our own prodigality. We have run away from God innumerable times into far countries of our own choosing where we have lived our lives the way we wanted to live them. Too often, it seems, that is the fact in our relationship with God that we know and understand with such clarity that it stops our ears from learning the lesson of this parable. What this parable is trying to tell us is that there is another aspect of our relationship to God that we ought to understand just as we understand our own prodigality and that is that God is a waiting and forgiving God; a God who forgives prodigal people. The waiting and forgiving character of God is the most important thing that we all have to learn from this text. Prodigal people become believing people, people of faith, when we understand and believe that God's forgiveness is a more important and a more dominant element in our relationship to God than is our own prodigality.

3

PROCLAMATORY PREACHING

WE WILL TURN OUR ATTENTION in this chapter to a second type of preaching: proclamatory preaching. As I defined the didactic type I underscored in a number of ways that didactic preaching, whether it is defined out of the Gutenberg galaxy or not, is a type of preaching that emphasizes cognition. The words associated with preaching of this type are, therefore, cognitive in nature. Preaching *informs* the hearer. It gets *points* and *lessons* across. It is sculpted in such a way that the hearer may understand the ideas that are being *explained*. The "massage" of didactic preaching is primarily a mental massage.

In describing proclamatory preaching we will use a different vocabulary. In this discussion we will characterize preaching as an *event*. We will talk about what *happens* through the preached word. Preaching will be described as dealing with the *reality* and *effect* of the gospel rather than its *ideas* and *content*.

I have indicated in the introduction that for clarity of discussion I would sharply divide my discussion of these three types of preaching. It is very important, on the one hand, to contrast these types with each other in as sharp a way as possible. On the other hand, I would ask you to be aware that in reality the sharpness of these divisions cannot be so clearly drawn. Didactic preaching may have elements of proclamation; proclamatory preaching is certainly not devoid of ideas, meaning, or content.

I have come to an understanding of proclamatory preaching from a variety of converging streams. The first important stream I should mention is usually called the new hermeneutic. Secondly, study of the Old Testament, and of the works of Gerhard von Rad, brought to my attention new ways of understanding how God's word functions in a dynamic, oral and creative manner in the Bible. The Bible so often associates God's spoken word with the word of *promise* that it is difficult to escape the reality that a word of promise carries within itself a *proclamation* of *fulfillment*. A third stream that was important for me in a personal odyssey that led me to the following description of proclamatory preaching was a new reading of the works of Martin Luther from the perspectives I had gained through the new hermeneutic and the biblical studies mentioned above. We will begin our discussion of proclamatory preaching from within the new hermeneutic with a brief section on the applicable insights of Rudolf Bultmann.

Rudolf Bultmann: The "Medium" Is the Message

In some of his writings Rudolf Bultmann represents proclamatory preaching in its most radical form. Preaching, for Bultmann, is anything but didactic! This can be illustrated by lifting out a few portions of Bultmann's pivotal and classic essay on the relation of myth and kerygma entitled, "New Testament and Mythology." [1]

Bultmann's famous essay deals with the encounter of the scientifically informed twentieth century mind with what he calls the "outdated," "mythological" world view of the New Testament. I realize, of course, that Bultmann did not write that essay in order to criticize didactic preaching! The essay could be read, however, as a critique of didactic preaching and as the espousal of a radically different understanding of preaching as proclamation.

One of the characteristics of didactic preaching we discussed was that it communicates to its hearer the truths of the Bible which the hearer, in turn, is called upon to believe. Bultmann is convinced that the world view in which the so-called truths of the New Testament are dressed has its origin in the mythological framework of Jewish Apocalyptic and Gnostic redeemer myths. For illustrative purpose let's use the resurrection of Jesus. Most people are aware that Bultmann does not believe that the resurrection of Jesus is a historical event in any way that we would normally understand historical events. Language which refers to the resurrection of Jesus may have made sense to people of Jewish background steeped in apocalyptic images or to people of Hellenistic background who expected the Gnostic redeemer to return to heaven from which he had come. It may make little sense, however, to people who live in the twentieth century, and who have a totally different view of the world. If we are asked to believe that such a resurrection is literally true then we are actually being asked to sacrifice our intellect in order to have faith. The faith called for by didactic preaching (faith as believing the truths of the Bible) is understood by Bultmann, therefore, to be faith as "the sacrifice of the intellect." The most faithful person would be the person who believed the greatest number of biblically unbelievable things to be true. For Bultmann such a view of faith has very little to do with the New Testament.

Bultmann's proposal is that we strip the myth from the kerygma (strip the outdated world views from the essential understanding of human existence) in order that in our preaching we might call people to genuine faith. Christian preaching and teaching should not lay unbelievable, outdated, mythological ideas on people and exhort them to believe them. The call to faith represented by Christian preaching is a call of a quite different nature.

Still using the resurrection as our example, Bultmann understands that the cross and resurrection of Jesus are a single, indivisible cosmic event that brings judgment to the world and opens us up for the possibility of authentic life. So indivisible are cross and resurrection in Bultmann's mind that he understands, "faith in the resurrection is really the same thing as faith in the saving efficacy of the cross. . . ." [2] It is when Bultmann asks how we come to believe in the saving efficacy of the cross that we catch his understanding of the relationship of faith, preaching and the resurrection. How do we come to believe?

> There is only one answer. This is the way in which the cross is proclaimed. It is always proclaimed together with the resurrection. Christ meets us in the preaching as one crucified and risen. He meets us in the word of preaching and nowhere else. The faith of Easter is just this—faith in the word of preaching.[3]

The resurrection of Jesus is not a historical event. It cannot be used as an objective event of history which proves that the cross is really true after all. Belief in Jesus of the cross as the risen one first occurred in the life of the disciples. But their faith cannot be the basis of our faith. We cannot believe in the resurrection either because it actually happened or because the disciples believed that it happened. "In the word of preaching and there alone we meet the risen Lord." [4] As far as Bultmann is concerned that is precisely what St. Paul meant when he wrote to the Romans: "So faith comes from what is heard, and what is heard comes by the preaching of Christ" (Rom. 10:17).

For Bultmann it is most certainly true that the *medium* (preaching) is the message/massage! The resurrection confronts us today solely as an event of preaching. We are called from death to life. We are called from old securities to the radical openness of God's eschatological future. That is a call that comes to us in our time and in our place through the oral proclamation of the preached word.

Bultmann presents us with a radically new understanding of preaching! Preaching is certainly not didactic. The preacher does not tell us all *about* the resurrection and then ask us to believe that it is true. Preaching is not about the task of asking us to believe that "unbelievable" things are true. Preaching does not call on us to believe in some objective events of history that are "out there" someplace. Preaching is never about some other time and some other place. Preaching is always a *present tense call* to the hearer to believe. The medium *is* the message. We are called to believe again today through this particular event of preaching. Christ meets us in the event of preaching and nowhere else! Christ always meets us in living words that call us to decision and participation in his life. Christ is present for us today in the event of preaching and in that event alone!

In this essay and in many other places in his writings Bultmann presents us with a radical new understanding of the dynamic task of preaching. When I begin my discussion in this chapter by discussing this radical new way of talking about preaching I do not do so as one who believes that Bultmann has given us the last word on the subject. As you will see in the course of our discussion I place a much more important significance on the historicity of the resurrection, for example, than Bultmann does. I don't agree with Bultmann's whole program! I do believe, however, that his discussion of kerygma, myth and the role of preaching is an excellent starting point for our thinking about proclamatory preaching.

The New Hermeneutic

Biblical interpretation in the first half of the twentieth century was dominated by what is often called the new hermeneutic. Rudolf Bultmann played a leading role in the development of this school of biblical understanding and interpretation. In an earlier chapter I indicated my belief that hermeneutics predisposes homiletics. Tell me how you understand Scripture and I think I can sketch a fairly clear picture of the kind of sermons you preach. A change in hermeneutics will therefore have an effect on the homiletical practices of its generation.

James M. Robinson and John B. Cobb Jr. have been the editors of a series of volumes on the new frontiers of twentieth century theology. One of those volumes presents an excellent summary discussion of the new hermeneutic. In a lengthy opening essay Robinson sketches the origin and development of this new hermeneutic.[5] The essay, of course, tells us of the important role played by Bultmann. It begins, however, with a discussion of the ways in which Karl Barth functioned as the catalytic agent in the hermeneutical change of the twentieth century.

Robinson begins his article by indicating that the new hermeneutic began when scholars understood that the language of the text is not simply language in need of interpretation.

> Rather than the language being a secondary, distorting objectification of meaning that must be removed to free the meaning behind the language, the language of the text is regarded positively as an interpretative proclamation of that meaning and hence as our indispensable access to it.[6]

Hermeneutics, therefore, shifted its focus. The primary task of hermeneutics was no longer conceived of as *explaining* the language of the text. Explaining a text is a didactic exercise. In McLuhan's language the emphasis is to shed "light on."

The new hermeneutic, according to Robinson, moved beyond the didactic, "light on" task of explaining the text. It moved to a "light through" way of thinking about texts. Texts were not simply to be explained. When explanation is the task then the exegete or interpreter of Scripture establishes a column of points of explanation and meaning *parallel* to the text itself. On a study work sheet it might look something like this:

TEXT	EXPLANATION (meaning)
Luke 15:1-7	
Now the tax collectors and sinners were all drawing near to him. And the Pharisees and the scribes murmured, saying, "This man receives sinners and eats with them."	1. Jesus' ministry was in constant tension with the religious leaders of his day.
	2. Sinners, not religious people, are the focus of Jesus' ministry.
So he told them this parable: "What man of you, having a hundred sheep, if he has lost one of them, does not	3. Jesus' attitude is a mirror of God's attitude.
	4. Etc.

leave the ninety-nine in the wilderness, and go after the one which is lost, until he finds it? And when he has found it, he lays it on his shoulders, rejoicing. And when he comes home, he calls together his friends and his neighbors, saying to them, "Rejoice with me, for I have found my sheep which was lost." Even so, I tell you there will be more joy in heaven over one sinner who repents than over ninety-nine righteous persons who need no repentance."

In contrast to this parallel way of juxtaposing text and explanation, the new hermeneutic sought to come to understanding *through* the text. In other words, the language of the text itself is a *bearer* of meaning. Meaning is not just something parallel or additional to the text. Meaning comes through the proclamatory character of the language of the text itself.

As far as Robinson is concerned the crucial turn in biblical hermeneutics came with Barth's commentary on *Romans.*

This book is not hermeneutics, a theory about interpretation, but rather hermeneia: a commentary, in which the subject matter of Paul's language is radically translated and proclaimed anew in the language of our day. It is this *fait accompli* that has called forth the hermeneutical reflection of our times.[7]

For our purposes the most important words out of that quotation are *proclaimed anew.* Barth sought to *proclaim* Paul's message to his own generation. He wasn't trying to *explain* what Paul means. He wasn't trying to give us a commentary full of the meaning in Paul's words. He actually wanted to have Paul say to us what he had said to the congregation at Rome some nineteen centuries earlier. Barth wanted us to hear Paul's word anew in our time.

According to Robinson, Barth, in setting out to have Paul's Romans message proclaimed anew, reversed the standard understanding of the relationship between subject and object in the exegetical (hermeneutical) task. The norm was that the exegete was understood as the *subject* who worked on the *object* (the text) in order to explain it. Though we did not use those words, that was our understanding of a didactic hermeneutic. The preacher as person (subject) masters the text (object) in order to pass along the objects of his discovery to the hearer via the preached word. Barth reverses this relationship between subject and object.

> . . . the flow of the traditional relation between subject and object, in which the subject interrogates the object, and, if he masters it, obtains from it his answer, has been significantly reversed. For it is now the object—which should henceforth be called the subject matter—that puts the subject in question.[8]

In other words, the text is no longer understood as an objective entity that I shape into sermonic form. It is no longer I who master the text. *The text masters me!* The text is the subject of address. The text addresses me. I am, so to speak, the object being addressed. The text is not to be understood as *dead* language in need of my explanations. The text should rather be understood as a word that is *alive*, a word that addresses me, calls my life into question and announces to me the gracious goodness of God. My understanding of proclamatory preaching is at least partially grounded in this new hermeneutic that views the text as a word that is alive (we return here to the pre-Gutenberg world of the spoken word) and proclamatory in nature.

There have been many practitioners of the new hermeneutic. Rudolf Bultmann, Gerhard Ebeling, and Ernst Fuchs are a few of the names that come to mind when the revolution in hermeneutics which Barth began is discussed. Each scholar has carved out his own niche in the field. One aspect of this hermeneutic was the new attention it paid to the character of language. Scholars like Fuchs and Ebeling talked about *language events*. Hybrid German words were created to make the new understanding of language clear. Fuchs used the term language event *(sprachereignis)* and Ebeling spoke of word-happenings *(wortgeschehen)*. In either case we see the oral character and power of language reasserting itself. Words do things. Words make things happen. Words have power over our lives.

The event character and/or the happening power of words is not just an interesting reality hatched by some ivory tower German scholars who like to play with words. It is an oral/aural fact in our everyday life. Words cause positive or negative responses in us. Fuchs and Ebeling and Bultmann are right. Words do have happening power. They have the power to change the whole course of a day, a week and, for some, an entire life.

The word-events that come hurtling into our lives can be bad news words or they can be good news words. Good news words range from the simple to the sublime. "That's a nice outfit you've got on today." "I really think your sermon last week was one of the best I've heard in my whole life." "I love you!" These are good news words! They affect us. We aren't the same having heard them. Words do have creative power. They can turn life around for us.

In a much more sophisticated way that is what the new hermeneutic is all about. The Bible is heard as a word-event or word-happening which takes a grip on our lives. The new hermeneutic listens to the word of God, the Bible, as a living word of *proclamation* which masters us, addresses us and creates new realities for our human existence.

Gerhard Ebeling: The Sermon Is Execution of the Text

In an article entitled, "Word of God and Hermeneutics," Gerhard Ebeling sets forth a summary of his understanding of the task of hermeneutics.[9] In the article he hopes to correct the customary view of hermeneutics as "the theory of the exposition of texts." That's the parallel columns approach we illustrated above. This customary view is that the language of a biblical text is language we must seek to understand and explain.

> This superficial view of understanding turns matters upside down and must therefore be completely reversed. *The primary phenomenon in the realm of understanding is not understanding of language, but understanding* through *language.* The word is not really the object of understanding, and thus the thing that poses the problem of understanding, the solution of which requires exposition and therefore also hermeneutics as the theory of understanding. Rather, the word is what opens up and mediates understanding, i.e. brings something to understanding. *The word itself has a hermeneutic function.* If the word-event takes place normally, i.e. according to its appointed purpose, then there is no need of any aid to understanding, but it is itself an aid to understanding.[10]

For Ebeling this perspective on language opens up at least three perspectives on the hermeneutical task. In the first place, hermeneutics in the traditional sense of seeking to understand the text is only necessary when there is something about the language of the text which hinders the word-event of the text from happening for us. In this case hermeneutics may serve the task of removing the obstacles for us so that the word itself may perform its work upon us.

Second, the task of hermeneutics is perceived to have far more to do with understanding language and the nature of word-events than it has to do with the content of the language. *"Hermeneutics as the theory of understanding must therefore be the theory of words."* [11]

Third, hermeneutics is not just interested in matters of form. Hermeneutics, rather, addresses itself directly to the word directly to the reality that seeks to come to understanding through the word.

Ebeling's discussion of the hermeneutical task is applicable so far to all texts. He, of course, is primarily interested in spelling out the nature and character of theological hermeneutics—hermeneutics that has to do with the Word of God. Please note that when Ebeling talks about the Word of God he thinks of *word* in relation to ears that hear, never to eyes that read.

> When the Bible speaks of God's Word, then it means here unreservedly word as word—word that as far as its word-character is concerned is completely normal, let us not hesitate to say: natural, oral word taking place between man and man. [12]

As we have already indicated, Ebeling's understanding of words, and particularly of God's word, is that they are *event-full.*

> Word is, taken strictly, happening word. . . . For ultimately the question as to the content and the power of words are identical. Word is therefore rightly under-

stood only when it is viewed as an event which—like love—involves at least two. The basic structure of word is therefore not statement—that is an abstract variety of the word-event—but appraisal, certainly not in the colourless sense of information, but in the pregnant sense of participation and communication.[13]

Elsewhere Ebeling writes of the character of the word:

The power of words as communication is by no means restricted to information and the increase of knowledge. The power of words as an event is that they can touch and change our very life. . . . So we do not get at the nature of words by asking what they contain, but by asking what they effect, what they set going, what future they disclose.[14]

It is Ebeling's conviction that the Gospel-word, the word proclaimed concerning Jesus, is the fundamental word-event for Christians. God's Word reaches us through a variety of biblical texts. It should be clear that Ebeling understands words in texts to be power-filled, event-full words. The aim of a text in his understanding is certainly not the communication of ideas, information, and data. Rather, the aim of a text is that its word-event character might happen for the contemporary hearer.

Ebeling puts it this way:

The process from text to sermon can therefore be characterized by saying: proclamation that has taken place is to become proclamation that takes place. This transition from the text to sermon is a transition from scripture to the spoken word. Thus the task prescribed here consists in making what is written into spoken word or, as we can now also say, in letting the text become God's Word again. . . . The sermon as a sermon is not exposition of the text as past proclamation, but is itself proclamation in the present—and that means, then, that *the sermon is execution of the text.*[15]

It will become apparent to the reader that my understanding of proclamatory preaching is dependent upon
many sources and that I am directly dependent upon
Ebeling's understanding of preaching as it is set forth in
this quotation. The Bible is a collection of materials that
were originally alive in the community of faith as living
words of oral proclamation. The task of preaching is to
enable proclamation that took place long ago and far away
to become proclamation for people again today. Preaching
enables the text to become God's Word again as a living,
oral event in the life of twentieth century people.

The sermon is execution of the text. Taken out of context that line usually draws a pretty good laugh! We have
all heard sermons (have we also all preached them?) that
murdered/executed the text. That, of course, is not what
Ebeling is getting at. "Execution" refers to the text coming alive in a new time and place. We "execute" the text
when people in our audience hear with their ears what an
earlier people heard with their ears. That is the character
of textual preaching.

Gustaf Wingren: "The Living Word" [16]

Gustaf Wingren, professor of theology at Lund, Swe-
den, has written a book which is fundamentally a theology
of preaching entitled, *The Living Word.* (The Swedish
title is *Predikan.*) His insights on the task and character
of preaching do not differ much from those of Gerhard
Ebeling even though Wingren has not reached his conclusions in consortium with those scholars who are primarily
associated with the new hermeneutic. Interestingly, Wingren sees his book as a polemic (". . . written in a mood
of some arrogance and sometimes in anger, I admit.")
against the anthropology inherent in Barth's understand-

ing of the hermeneutical task. Barth, says Wingren, always understood the Word of God as something hurled *against* man.

> It must be possible to adhere to the belief in creation, to the continuity between the human and the Christian, to the view of salvation as a restoration of the natural and at the same time make room for what is justified in Barth's position—the interpretation of the Bible as direct address, as the Word now preached.[17]

The Word of God, in other words, is not a word hurled against us in our humanity a la Barth. It is, rather, the word that offers to us the gift of our humanity.

One of the fundamental aspects of Wingren's approach to preaching is his attempt to understand and set forth the proper relationship between God's Word and human existence. Wingren thinks that we have trouble understanding the Word of God and the task of preaching because we have not understood the indispensable connection between God's Word and human life. We have tended to see these realities as having an *independent* existence. The Word of God exists. Human life exists. The task facing the preacher has traditionally been thought of as bringing these two independently existing realities into relationship with each other in the sermon.

Such thinking lays tremendous burdens on ourselves as preachers. It is a burden because it becomes the task of preaching to get the Word and human beings together. As preachers, therefore, we must know the Word as well as possible. We must know our people equally well. If we are Spirit-filled or spiritual, perhaps we can pull off the task. But wherever such an understanding of the task and responsibility of preaching exists we should not be surprised to find that the pastor has ulcers!

Wingren challenges this understanding of the independent existence of the Word and people. The Word of God, according to Wingren, does not exist by itself. It exists to be heard; it exists in order to be proclaimed to people. A Bible sitting on a shelf is of absolutely no use. The Bible's word is useful and creative only as people read and hear. *The Word of God exists for people to hear.*

In a moment we shall examine the biblical support for Wingren's dynamic understanding of the Word of God. First we need to complete the dialectic relationship he sets forth. Human life does not exist by itself any more than God's Word exists by itself. Preaching is not preaching aimed at self-sufficient human life seeking to add something religious or spiritual to it. We come to God's Word as bound and conquered human beings in order to hear the word which sets our humanity free. We come to hear the word that gives us our human existence. *To be human is to hear God's Word that creates us, re-creates us and sets us free for human life.*

Now we have a quite different equation and a quite different perspective on the task of preaching and the preacher. God's Word exists in order to be heard. Human beings have true humanity when they hear God's Word addressed to them. Preaching, therefore, is not the ulcer-making task of trying to get God's Word and people together. Preaching is the joyful task of proclaiming God's Word in order to offer truly human life to all who hear. God's Word and human life are *interdependent* realities, not independently existing realities.

Wingren's concept of the homiletical task relies on a certain way of looking at God's Word. When we in the Christian tradition use the phrase "Word of God" almost all ears immediately assume that we are talking about the Bible. That may be true. The Bible is the Word of God.

But Jesus Christ is also called the Word of God. He is the Word made flesh and dwelling among us. And, even before God's Word was made flesh in Jesus of Nazareth the people of the biblical tradition had a long history of understanding "Word of God" as the oral and creative words that came forth from the mouth of God. And God *said*, "Let there be light" (Gen. 1). God spoke. That is clearly a reference to an *oral* word. There was light! God's oral word had creative power.

This understanding of God's Word as oral and creative is the fundamental biblical understanding of the Word of God. Jesus as the Word of God and Bible as the Word of God prove that God's Word is fundamentally oral and creative. The first chapter of Genesis is full of the phrase, "God said." He even said, "Let us make man in our image. . . ." *We exist because God spoke!* God spoke us into being.

The finest statement of the character of God's Word is recorded in Isaiah:

> For as the rain and the snow come down from heaven,
> and return not thither but water the earth,
> making it bring forth and sprout,
> giving seed to the sower and bread to the eater,
> so shall my word be that goes forth from my mouth;
> it shall not return to me empty,
> but it shall accomplish that which I purpose,
> and prosper in the thing for which I sent it (Isa. 55:10-11).

The words that go forth from the mouth of God always accomplish something. They fulfill God's intended purposes. That is good news for us. It is good news because we live by every word that comes forth from the mouth of God.

> . . . man does not live by bread alone, but . . . by everything that proceeds out of the mouth of the Lord (Deut. 8:3).

When Jesus was tempted by the devil to live his life out of his own strength and power by turning stones to bread, Jesus quoted this Old Testament passage. Jesus knew what human life was all about. It is not life that we possess independently; life to use as we please. Human life is life-in-dependence on every word that comes forth from the mouth of God.

St. John seems to tell us that Jesus himself came forth from the mouth of God. "In the beginning was the Word, and the Word was with God, and the Word was God. He was in the beginning with God. . . . In him was life. . . ." (John 1:1-4) When Jesus is proclaimed to me through human words or through the pages of Scripture I hear the word that proceeds from God's mouth. I hear the word that gives me my life. When I go to church and listen to the preacher present God's Word I receive my life from God anew. Preaching participates in God's word-event. Through preaching I hear God's life-giving word spoken to me today. *Jesus is spoken into my life by the proclamation of the preacher.* That's what I understand Wingren to be driving at in his attempt to grasp the meaning of the Word of God in relationship to human existence.

In order to comprehend what Wingren wants to say about preaching one must understand clearly his depiction of the human dilemma. Human life is less than human in Wingren's mind, because it is *conquered* life. His view of sin is that our lives are held captive by alien and demonic powers. Captive and conquered human nature needs to hear the word of Jesus, the word of cross and resurrection, as the word that sets it free for restored human life. The word Jesus addressed to people in his earthly ministry set them free from their captivity to sin, blindness, deafness, death, etc. We hear and proclaim that same word today. Our experience of captivity is fundamentally the same as that of Jesus' hearers. The word of freedom he spoke to them, therefore, strikes our ears in the same way. Preaching brings that word of Jesus which releases us from captivity and restores us to natural human life.

Wingren sees Jesus as the one locked in conflict with all the powers that would bind us to something less than full human life. In a footnote he outlines the role of preaching relying heavily on the premise of conflict.

(a) The Bible tells of ordinary, factual history which has the characteristic of a conflict.

(b) The conflict has not reached its end with the end of the Bible.

(c) To the continuation of that conflict preaching belongs as the present stage of God's redemptive action in history.

(d) To preach or to hear someone preach is to take one's place within the long chain of Biblical acts; to give up preaching, on the contrary, is to drop the link from the chain which clips the present part to the part that precedes preaching—and a chain with a missing link is no longer whole, is not a 'unity.'

(e) The conflict of Biblical history will be unfinished even when preaching comes to an end; it will only be complete in the resurrection of the dead and the last judgment.[18]

Wingren's outline of the task of preaching is self-explanatory. I would like to expand briefly, however, on point (c) in his outline. Preaching, he writes, is, " . . . the present stage of God's redemptive action in history." At the beginning of human history God called life into existence through his powerful, creative word. That history will be called to an end by "the voice of the Son of God" (John 5:25-29), by the Lord's "cry of command" (1 Thess 4:16). Human life and history is surrounded by

God's Word. God's Word is the alpha and omega of our existence.

But God's Word also comes into history and into our individual lives in the time between his alpha-word and his omega-word. The Bible bears witness that God comes to his people between alpha and omega words as the one who spoke promises to Israel. Those promises were fulfilled. They found their highest fulfillment in Jesus Christ: God's Word-made-flesh. To people in the twentieth century God's Word comes as the word of preaching. God spoke to patriarch and prophet. God spoke in and through the person of Jesus Christ. God speaks to us through the words of preaching that bear faithful witness to his words of promise and his word-made-flesh. *Preaching is the present stage of God's redemptive action in history.* That statement from Wingren appears to me to be almost precisely parallel to Ebeling's, "the sermon is the execution of the text."

Martin Luther: Pause Here and Let Him Do You Good

Wingren's book on preaching is dependent at points on Martin Luther. This led me to a rereading of Luther to see if Wingren's usage was correct. Luther has been quoted on both sides of the question of the nature of the Bible or the Word of God. He has been quoted in support of a static view of the Word: verbal inspiration. He has been quoted in support of a dynamic view of the Word. Will the real Martin Luther please stand up?

My rereading has convinced me that Luther, indeed, has a dynamic view of the Word of God and that he understands the Word as an oral and creative word in much the way Wingren claims. It is not possible to document the case for this reading of Luther extensively in this place. But these selections confirm the observation that, "When one meets the phrase 'Word of God' in Luther's writings, it usually has reference to this oral word of proclamation." [19]

> Luther lays great stress on the fact that the Gospel is a spoken word, not primarily a book, but a Word that is heralded abroad. The Gospel is "a good message." "It is really not what is found in books and what is spelled out with letters but rather an oral preaching, a living Word, a voice which sounds into all the world, and is openly heralded forth, so that it may be heard everywhere." That Gospels had to be written was itself a weakness, "a great quenching of the Spirit." When that took place it was not intended that written material should replace the earlier spoken word but, on the contrary, that the spoken word should be able to continue thanks to their accounts: "The Gospel is, and cannot be other than, the account of the story of Christ." [20]

In Ebeling's *Word and Faith* we read the following quotation from Luther:

> Christ himself did not write his teaching, as Moses did his, but delivered it orally, also commanded to deliver it orally and gave no command to write it. . . . For that reason it is not at all the manner of the New Testament to write books of Christian doctrine, but there should everywhere, without books, be good, learned, spiritually-minded, diligent preachers to draw the living word from the ancient scriptures and constantly bring it to life before the people, as the apostles did. For before ever they wrote, they had preached to and converted the people by word of mouth, which also was their real apostolic and New Testament work. [21]

> And the Gospel should not really be something written, but a spoken word which brought forth the Scriptures, as Christ himself did not write anything but only spoke. He called his teaching not Scripture but gospel, meaning

good news or a proclamation that is spread not by pen but by word of mouth. So we go on and make the gospel into a law book, a teaching of commandments, changing Christ into a Moses, the One who would help us into simply an instructor.[22]

I would like to have you pay particular attention to that last quote from Luther. He issues a warning. We must not turn the gospel (the oral proclamation of good news) into a law book (a written word). If we do that we will lose the whole mission and message of Christ. If Christ is simply someone we read about in a book like the books that Moses wrote (Luther assumed Mosaic authorship of the Pentateuch), then Christ becomes just another instructor. If Christ becomes locked in a book as a didactic lesson for us, the Christ of the New Testament disappears. Christ is the one who presented himself to people in order to help them, to do something for them, to release them from captivity. In like manner Christ should come to us as the one who can help us in our life situations. The proclamation of the gospel concerns Christ as the one who helps us. Preaching is not intended to point to a book in which we can learn about help from an Instructor Christ. *Preaching offers people help; it does not teach them that Christ is a helper.*

Luther's debate with Zwingli over the character of the real presence of Christ in the Eucharist is well known. One of the arguments he uses against Zwingli is the argument from preaching. "I preach the gospel of Christ, and with my bodily voice I bring Christ into your heart. . . ." Luther evidently assumes that Zwingli understands and accepts this powerful view of preaching. That being the case Zwingli should have no difficulty comprehending what Luther wishes to say about the eucharistic real presence. His argument goes like this:

> Now I can accomplish this again, that the one Christ en-
> ters into so many hearts through the voice, and that each
> person who hears the sermon and accepts it takes the
> whole Christ into his heart. . . . Now see, as I have said,
> how much the poor bodily voice is able to do. First of all
> it brings the whole Christ to the ears; then it brings him
> into the hearts of all who listen and believe. Should it
> then be so amazing that he enters into the bread and
> wine? [23]

We would certainly be justified in calling Luther's view
of preaching *sacramental.*

What an astonishing view of preaching and the use
God makes of the bodily voice! Through our voices,
through our oral proclamation, Christ comes to the ears
and hearts of those who hear and believe. The Christ
Luther wishes to proclaim is certainly not an instructor!
When the whole Christ is formed within the hearts of
those who hear then Christ is present within their very
bodies *in order to help them.*

I have said a number of times that hermeneutics predisposes homiletics. In another place Luther confirms this
observation by running his view of hermeneutics and
homiletics together in what to me is an extremely helpful statement of the issue.

> When you open the book containing the gospels and read
> or hear how Christ comes here or there, or how someone
> is brought to him, you should therein perceive the ser-
> mon or the gospel through which he is coming to you,
> or you are being brought to him. For the preaching of
> the gospel is nothing else than Christ coming to us, or
> we being brought to him. When you see how he works,
> however, and how he helps everyone to whom he comes or
> who is brought to him, then rest assured that faith is
> accomplishing this in you and that he is offering your
> soul exactly the same sort of help and favor through the
> gospel. If you pause here and let him do you good, that

is, if you believe that he benefits and helps you, then you really have it. Then Christ is yours, presented to you as a gift.[24]

The hermeneutic here is that of *pausing before a text* in order that Christ may do for us in our time what he did for those in the text. Christ is our helper; he is not just one who instructs us in the lesson of help. Pausing before a text is the same reality as pausing before the preached word. Through the Word of God, written and proclaimed, Christ comes to us to do us good! *Christ himself is present doing his work through preaching.* That is Luther's understanding of the hermeneutical and the homiletical task. In formulating my own understanding of proclamatory preaching I stand in Luther's debt. Proclamatory preaching is cradled in the assumption that preached words bring Christ as helper into the lives of all who pause before that word in order that Christ may do them good.

Characteristics of Proclamatory Preaching

It is now time to draw together the strands of our discussion and to set forth the characteristics of proclamatory preaching. These characteristics are listed in a manner parallel to the characteristics of didactic preaching. It is hoped that this parallel listing will make it easier for you to see the similarities and differences between these two types. The characteristics of proclamatory preaching are:

- the goal of preaching is that the good news of the gospel be proclaimed in such a way that it happens in the life of the hearer.
- the biblical text comes alive again for the hearer.
- the sermon is aimed at sinful human beings.

- the development of the sermon should seek to enable proclamation that took place to become proclamation that takes place.
- the sermon seeks to enhance the oral character of the Word.
- the faith engendered in the hearer is faith created by a living encounter with God's Word.

1. *The goal of preaching is that the good news of the gospel be proclaimed in such a way that it happens in the life of the hearer.* In describing the aim of didactic preaching I told the story of young lovers who learned all *about* love. Proclamatory preaching on the other hand is analogous to what lovers really *do* when they meet. Lovers gaze at each other, touch each other, speak to each other. "I love you," they whisper. Lovers proclaim good news to each other. They don't read books about love or talk about or become experts in the concept of love.

It ought to be the same with preaching. Preachers proclaim good news to their hearers. "Jesus loves you." "You are loved by the maker of heaven and earth." "In Jesus' name I am bold to say to you, 'I love you.' " *Preachers proclaim good news* in proclamatory preaching. They don't give sermons *about* good news.

Forgiveness of sins is one of the fundamental realities of the Christian faith and, therefore, one of the fundamental subjects of preaching. In proclamatory preaching forgiveness is offered, announced, proclaimed to people. At some point in the sermon we speak to people on God's behalf. "Your sins are forgiven." We speak that powerful, creative word of God to people. It is not our word. We are not speaking on our own authority. We speak in the name of another. We speak in the name of Jesus Christ. The word of forgiveness, Christ's word of forgiveness, which comes forth from our mouth and enters the ears and hearts of our listeners creates exactly what it announces. People are forgiven. Such is the power of preaching!

One of my colleagues said that the pastor must "believe in God for others." At first I didn't understand what he meant. Surely other people can't be saved by my faith! That was not what he meant. He meant to say that as a preacher I must have some fundamental kind of confidence that God is *for* others. I cannot announce a word of forgiveness in my sermon unless I believe that God really intends to forgive all these people sitting before me. That's easier said than believed. Pastors know their people pretty well. Many of those people don't really seem to *deserve* to hear God's forgiving word. The character of the gospel, however, pushes us to make that public announcement of forgiveness. Jesus Christ shows us the heart of God. It is a heart of love for the fallen, sinful people of this earth. That love and forgiveness is what we proclaim on Sunday morning. Without a strong belief that God is *for* other people, proclamatory preaching would be impossible!

If I were to make a theological conclusion on this subject based on my experiences I would have to say that preachers of the Word seem to find it easier to believe that God's ordinances and commands are *for* others than to believe that God's mercy and love are *for* others. I am often questioned and challenged on my strong convictions that preaching ought to announce a word of *public absolution* (in Lutheran circles preaching would be understood as the public exercise of the Office of the Keys) to the gathered assembly. Those who challenge me, however, do not hesitate to publicly proclaim that God makes demands on us, has set forth his commandments for us to keep and challenges us to live out his laws. It seems quite natural and wise to believe in the universal applicability of God's law. It seems unnatural and foolish, on the other hand, to believe that God's love and forgiveness are just as universally applicable. We need to be reminded here of Paul's assertion that it pleases God to save those who believe through the folly of what we preach. (See 1 Cor. 1:18-26.) The folly of what we preach is that God is *for* all others as a God of compassion and forgiveness.

Another way of describing the dynamics of proclamatory preaching is by making it clear that in this form of preaching the preacher must almost always, at some point in the sermon, speak in first or second person, present tense language. Entire sermons on forgiveness can be couched in third person, past-tense language. We can talk about the fact that *Jesus* (that's third person: he) *forgave* (that's past tense) sinners. That's not proclamation! That's information.

First person, present tense language would say: "In the name of Jesus Christ *I* (first person) *say* (present tense) to you: 'Your sins are forgiven.' " Second person, present tense language would go like this: "Jesus says (present tense) to you this morning, 'Your (second person) sins are forgiven.' " That's proclamation.

The same format of first or second person, present tense language can be used in preaching to announce the event character of most biblical metaphors. In Jesus name we can make a number of present tense proclamations:

> In Jesus' name I tell you this day—
> you *are* justified by his grace.
> you *are* the children of God.

you *are* redeemed.
you *have* eternal life.

This first person speaking on our part has some interesting biblical models. Jacob robbed his brother Esau of his birthright and blessing. He fled the land in fear of his brother's wrath. When he was about to return he sent messengers before him to Esau with a message. He instructed them, ". . . 'Thus you shall say to my lord Esau: Thus says your servant Jacob, "I have sojourned with Laban . . ."'" (Gen. 32:1-5). Note that the messenger was to speak for Jacob in the first person, "*I* have sojourned. . . ." This is evidently a typical way of communicating a message in an oral culture. I think it is also a legitimate way to think about the oral task of preaching. When we preach we, too, speak on behalf of another!

The aim of proclamatory preaching is to create an event, to make something happen for the hearer. Through our words of proclamation forgiveness happens, justification happens, redemption happens for those who hear and believe.

2. *The biblical text comes alive again for the hearer.* Proclamatory preaching strives to "execute" the text. In our preparation for preaching we must first pause before that text and let it speak to us in its totality. What happens to us through the language of this text? When we have been mastered by the text, when it has spoken to us, then we are ready to start our sermon preparation. The question we have in our minds as we go about the task of constructing a sermon is, "How can I preach on this text in such a way that what happened to me through this text may also happen to the congregation." We can put that kind of question to the text in a different manner. "What happened to those people who first encountered

this parable, miracle story, etc.? How can I re-create that happening for my hearers?"

In either case we operate under the assumption that the Word is the subject of address to its hearers. The Word spoke to people of old; the same Word speaks to me and to other people today. The sermon is the oral instrument through which the Word happens again for people.

There is another hermeneutical assumption at work here. We assume that the Spirit of God is at work in and through ("light through") this text speaking to people. Biblical texts speak to the hopes, dreams, fears and anxieties of human beings. As preachers we don't have to rework the text so that it will speak to the needs of people as we understand them. (Surely there are times and texts when this is necessary.) We can normally assume that the text is relevant. If we can somehow help this text come alive again the Holy Spirit will drive the reality of the text into the reality of the human lives now confronted by the text.

3. *The sermon is aimed at sinful human beings.* The human condition is a sinful condition. However you chose to express the reality of sinful human existence it is a reality that the preacher must never forget as the sermon is prepared and the pulpit entered. The faces of the people looking up at us are always the faces of sinful people. Preaching can run into two fundamental dangers at this point. The first is the age-old danger of judgmentalism. We judge people in the pew by what we see externally and wonder if we can really believe that God is for them. Surely God doesn't tolerate such people in his kingdom!

When we fall victim to the judgmental danger we may actually withhold the liberating word of the gospel. Jesus

Christ comes to people through the words of our preaching. Some texts communicate Jesus' words of judgment. Most New Testament texts communicate Jesus' words of liberation. Our preaching should remain faithful to the texts before us. (Those who preach in a tradition where the texts for Sunday are appointed are fortunate at this point I believe.) We may communicate the text by dividing it into those parts which are words of judgment and those parts which are words of liberation for sinful people. We divide the texts. We should not divide the people! That is, we should not decide that certain people need to hear words of judgment and certain people need to hear words of liberation no matter what the text might say. At that point I believe we must trust that as we give oral rebirth to the biblical texts, God's Spirit will use those words to bring the reality of judgment or liberation as he sees fit. Determining who needs to hear words of judgment and who needs to hear words of liberation is the Spirit's job, not ours!

The second danger that preaching often runs into in the area of human sinfulness is that it spends too much time describing what it means to be sinful and excoriating people for it. A Lutheran pastor once told me that he was taught to spend the first part of his sermon preaching the law (describing, analyzing and scolding people for their sins) and the second part of his sermon preaching the gospel (the word that liberates them from their sinfulness). That advice appears to me to have a number of flaws. The most obvious is that preaching would be spending at least half of its time telling people what they already know! People know they are caught in life; they know they are sinners. They know the contours of their sinfulness much better than we do. What they come to hear from us is a word that sets them free. They come to hear us say, "In the name of Jesus I say to you, 'You are free!'"

Because people know the shape of their own predicament better than we do there is another flaw in this half law and half gospel formula. I think many sermons wind up preaching the law in ways that most people do not experience in life. As we would hear this particular sermon, therefore, we would hear a description of human sin that is unfamiliar to us. We hear a new problem presented. But it is not necessarily our problem. Then we hear the gospel. The new problem is solved. So we have a new problem and a new solution. But we go home with the same set of problems that we came to church with!

We are better off, I think, assuming that people know and feel where life catches them up. They experience life as caught and bound people. (It is often helpful, however, to give the expression in preaching to the sense of bondage that people experience.) People in bondage are anxious to hear a word of freedom. Jesus is that word of freedom. Our proclamation brings Jesus, brings freedom, to our hearers. Through our proclamatory words, Jesus sets sinful people free. Proclamatory preaching seeks to bring people to the text that they might hear the text's liberating address.

4. *The development of the sermon should seek to enable proclamation that took place to become proclamation that takes place.* For the structural development of the sermon this will mean different things for different texts. As far as possible the structural development of a given sermon should take the form that best suits a particular text. We need freedom from the pre-set mold syndrome that occurs when we have a particular format or outline that we apply to each text we work with. I know whereof

I speak! For almost 15 years of my ministry that is exactly what I did. I had learned one style of sermonic outline which I used for just about every sermon I preached. I had a pre-set mold!

The pre-set mold I used was not inherently bad—in fact, it was quite good. I learned it this way:

Theme:

Introduction

I.   (First main point)
     A.
     B.

II.
     A.
     B.

III.
     A.
     B.

Conclusion

I assumed that every biblical text could fit that mold. That's a false assumption. Each biblical text has its peculiar literary form. If we wish to enable these ancient proclamatory texts to become living proclamation for people today we must pay attention to the peculiar form of each text. The development of a proclamatory sermon (perhaps of any sermon!) should stand in some kind of organic relationship to the structure of the text itself.

I would like to present a couple of other molds that could be used in place of the one I learned. I present them in order to show that there are other possibilities. The mold or outline you use for a given sermon should not necessarily be chosen from the examples I give. Through thinking about a variety of developmental possibilities you should find ways to create a mold that fits the text you wish to bring to living proclamation.

a. Many Paths to the Center

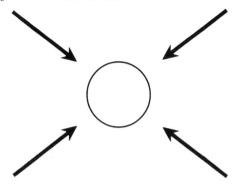

A sermon can be thought of as having a living center of proclamation. The paths to that center, the paths on which we lead people in order that they may hear the living word of the text, may come at that center from many directions.

b. Circling and Expanding the Center

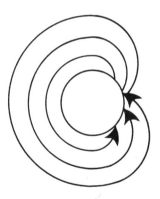

Here again the sermon has a living center. The development of the center moves out in ever expanding circles always returning to the center. The sermon structure looks something like what we see when a pebble is thrown into a brook. The pebble creates a ripple effect. As we watch the center, that spot where the pebble entered water, is always there. Our eyes don't lose sight of the center but the radiating effects of that center expand ever outward. Proclamatory preaching can, likewise, radiate outward from a dynamic, living center.

c. A Single Center or Climax

Where preaching time is sparse the sermon may simply cover whatever biblical and contemporary material the preacher wishes to include and move toward a single climax. Most texts have a single emphasis. The three-point sermon necessarily distorts that emphasis. There is certainly nothing wrong with a well-developed one-point sermon!

d. Homily

In seminary I learned that a homily was a way of preaching whereby the preacher "walked through" the text with the listener verse by verse. A homily, in other words, was a step by step unfolding of the text. It is obvious that a homily, understood in this way, is a kind of preaching that is faithful to the text. Some preachers may really be able to bring a text alive in this manner. It sounds easy. On the contrary, it takes inordinate communication skills to preach a homily and make it live.

e. Story

In Chapter 5 we will pursue the character of story preaching in detail.

We conclude, therefore, that there are a number of preaching styles and methodologies. In proclamatory preaching we should be sensitive to the text and seek to find a methodology of communication that enables proclamation that took place to become proclamation that takes place.

5. *The sermon seeks to enhance the oral character of the Word.* We discussed the importance of the sermon as oral communication under the characteristics of didactic preaching in Chapter 1. You may wish to review that material.

Proclamatory preaching is particularly reliant on good oral style. Our discussion throughout this chapter has been about living words, sermons as "execution" of texts, Christ coming to our ears through preaching, the bodily voice as the bearer of the reality of the gospel. Preaching brings a living word to human ears. It brings the living word of the gospel, the word that is Jesus Christ. The Bible itself unfolds for us the oral character of God's word and the creative power of that word. Preaching is a re-presentation of that word for contemporary hearing and for new creative possibilities.

This living word simply does not strike people as living when they listen to the preacher reading a manuscript. When we have an important message to bring to other human beings we don't read it! We announce it. ("I love you.") We proclaim it. ("The war is over!") We shout it. ("We won!") We whisper it. ("Your mother passed away this morning.") Preaching has a still more important message to be orally proclaimed. "Jesus Christ has set you free. You are free." That message should be announced, proclaimed, shouted and whispered. Our human voices bring incredibly good news to people in bondage to sin. We bring it with a twinkle in our eye, a dance in our step and emotion in our voice. Preaching is oral proclamation!

6. *The faith engendered in the hearer is faith created by a living encounter with God's Word.*

> But how are men to call upon him in whom they have not believed? And how are they to believe in him of whom they have never heard? And how are they to hear without a preacher? . . . So faith comes from what is heard, and what is heard comes by the preaching of Christ.
> —Rom. 10:14, 17.

Preaching participates in the creative power of God's Word. When God spoke, something happened. When God spoke, the world came to be. When God spoke, human life came to be. When God spoke in Christ, crippled people walked. When God spoke in Christ the deaf heard, the lame received their sight, prisoners were set free, sinners were forgiven, the dead returned to life. When we speak (preach) for God in Christ something happens. On behalf of God's Son we speak freedom and people are free. On behalf of God's Son we speak forgiveness and people are forgiven. On behalf of God's Son we speak resurrection and people are alive unto eternity.

We preach. Something happens. The preached word has the power to create what it announces. It doesn't have that power because we are the ones speaking. It has that power because God has that power and we speak His Word.

What is faith? Faith almost always gets its shape in dependence on our understanding of the Word of God. If God's Word is basically understood as a book containing all the truths about God, faith is understood as belief in those truths. If God's Word is understood to be that book which tells us all about Jesus and his love, faith is that human activity which chooses to believe in Jesus and his love. If the Word of God is understood to be an oral, creative word which creates what it announces, faith is understood to be *a living trust that what that Word has announced to us is the new reality of our life.*

As those who listen to preaching we hear that we are forgiven, that we are free, that we have eternal life. God's Word, that word present in preaching, has the power to create what it announces. If I hear that I am forgiven, I am forgiven. If I hear that I am free, I am free. If I hear that I have eternal life, I have eternal life. I have it because God has spoken it and God's Word has the power to bring to pass what it speaks.

Faith comes from what is heard. I have heard some good news about my life. I have heard it through preaching. The word I have heard is true. I am a different person because of it. I believe that. I believe that God's Word has the power to make my life new. I believe that I am forgiven, free and eternally full of God's life. I believe it because I have heard myself addressed with power-filled words. Faith comes from what is heard. To have faith is to believe that the words of God, the words of the Bible, the words of preaching which have penetrated my existence are true. Faith is trust in the creative word of God. It is engendered in me through a living encounter with God's Word. Proclamatory preaching calls people to believe that what they *hear* (God's Word) and not what they *see* (their own spiritual condition) is the reality of their life before God.

I take this to be a very high and serious view of preaching. Faith comes from what is heard, that is, preaching is an instrument for creating faith. Preaching creates faith when it is true to its task, "And what is heard comes by the preaching of Christ."

Afterword

It should be abundantly clear by now that I am enthusiastic about proclamatory preaching. Proclamatory preaching of the gospel gets closer to the heart of who Jesus is for us today. Proclaimed, he comes to me in my life situation through the words of preaching to justify me, make me righteous, forgive my sins and grant me the gift of eternal life.

There are some problems, however, with this type of preaching. In the first place, not all texts are proclamatory in nature. "Proclamation that took place becomes proclamation that takes place." We used that dictum from Gerhard Ebeling in describing proclamatory preaching. It would be very difficult, however, to discover the proclamatory character that took place in the original setting of some texts. Proclamation is simply not the aim or goal of every biblical text. Some texts are primarily texts of exhortation. Others have a more didactic character. Textual preaching should be true to the texts being preached. Not every text can be poured into a pre-set type called proclamatory preaching!

In the second place, proclamatory preaching has a highly *personal* and *individual* character. The gospel of Jesus Christ is certainly a personal message addressed to each person's individual existence. But the gospel also has *social* and *corporate* dimensions. The gospel addresses me and announces, "You are justified." God's justification of individual sinners, however, cannot be separated from God's concern with justice for all the peoples of earth. We can see that same relationship in the biblical metaphors of righteousness and peace. "You are righteous," the gospel announces. "You are at peace with God," it declares. That's the individualized side of the message.

Again, however, we know that God also seeks to create righteous relationships in society. He is interested in peace not just as the individual condition of my being but as the environment in which all people may dwell. An accent on proclamatory preaching must not lose sight of the social/corporate dimension of the gospel.

One final word to those whose preaching takes place in churches that celebrate the Lord's Supper frequently and who believe in some form of the "real presence" of Christ in that Supper. The "real presence" of Christ is a presence promised through oral words of proclamation. Each communicant hears an oral word of proclamatory promise: "The body of Christ, given for you. The blood of Christ, shed for you." How much easier the task of preaching (proclamatory preaching) is on Sundays when the Lord's Supper is served! On those days the sermon does not have to bear the whole weight of proclamation. Promissory words will be addressed to each parishioner at the table. The sermon can simply serve as an invitation to the meal, an invitation to the words of proclamation there to be announced. My own experience of attending worship on Lord's Supper Sundays indicates to me that pastors do not take nearly enough advantage of the eucharistic words of proclamation that are to follow their sermon. Sermon and Supper should form an organic whole.

Notes

1. Rudolf Bultmann, "New Testament and Mythology," in *Kerygma and Myth*, ed. Hans Werner Bartsch (New York and Evanston: Harper & Row, 1961).
2. Ibid., 41.
3. Ibid.
4. Ibid., 43.

5. James M. Robinson, "Hermeneutic Since Barth," in *New Frontiers in Theology,* Vol. II, eds., James M. Robinson and John B. Cobb, Jr. (New York: Harper and Row, 1964).
6. Ibid., 6-7.
7. Ibid., 22.
8. Ibid., 23-24.
9. Gerhard Ebeling, "Word of God and Hermeneutics," in *Word and Faith* (Philadelphia: Fortress, 1963).
10. Ibid., 318.
11. Ibid., 319.
12. Ibid., 325.
13. Ibid., 326.
14. Gerhard Ebeling, *The Nature of Faith* (Philadelphia: Fortress, 1967) 186-187.
15. Ibid., 329, 331.
16. Gustaf Wingren, *The Living Word* (London: SCM, 1960).
17. Gustaf Wingren, *The Flight from Creation* (Minneapolis: Augsburg, 1971), 20-21.
18. Wingren, *The Living Word,* 46.
19. Helmut T. Lehmann, gen. ed., *Luther's Works,* 54 vols., Companion Volume, *Luther the Expositor,* by Jaroslav Pelikan (St. Louis: Concordia, 1959), 63-64.
20. Wingren, *The Living Word,* 64.
21. Ebeling, *Word and Faith,* 312.
22. Helmut T. Lehmann, gen. ed., *Luther's Works,* 54 vols., vol. 35, *Word and Sacrament I,* ed. E. Theodore Bachmann (Philadelphia: Muhlenberg, 1960) 123.
23. Helmut T. Lehmann, gen. ed., *Luther's Works,* 54 vols., vol. 36, *Word and Sacrament II,* ed. Abdel Ross Wentz (Philadelphia: Muhlenberg, 1959) 340-341.
24. Ibid., 121.

4

PROCLAMATORY SERMONS

This chapter contains two proclamatory sermons. The relationship between these sermons and my description of proclamatory preaching should be self-evident. Hopefully they are faithful to the characteristics I have set forth.

The first sermon on Luke 15:11-32 will describe the sinful human condition more thoroughly than I recommended in Chapter 3. In trying to bring this text to life again for people I sought to create a living interface between the prodigal's prayer upon his return and the father's word of welcome. In seeking to create this interface, which struck me as a legitimate way of coming to grips with the center of this story, human bondage to sin received a good deal of time and attention.

There is congregational involvement and participation in this sermon. What is done here in this respect certainly cannot be done in every sermon. There is a problem in some white protestant churches with a lack of involvement on the part of people. This sermon represents one attempt to involve them physically, orally and aurally. We need to be on the look-out for imaginative ways of involving people in our sermons.

I have tried to write the sermons in this chapter the way that I would preach them. The oral character is retained in print. If a sentence or two strikes you as awkward as you read it try "hearing" it.

The Word of the Father

Luke 15:11-32

Introduction

The Prodigal Son.
  We know the story.
    We've heard it often.
      "Give me the share of property that falls to me."
        He got it.
His father gave it to him
  and away he went
    to a far country.
      He lived it up,
        but not for long.
          The funds ran dry.
            What to do?
              You don't have many choices when you're
              desperate.
                He wound up feeding swine!
"There's got to be a better way," he thought.
"My father's hired servants are better off than I am."
"That's it! I'll go home. Maybe my father will make me
one of his hired servants.

God knows it's better than feeding swine."
He'd go home.
But would he be received?
Would his father have him back at all?
The prodigal didn't know the answer to that
question.
But he hoped.
And he prayed.
He had his confessional prayer ready
to go:
"Father, I have sinned against heaven and before you.
I am no longer worthy to be called your son."

Part One: The Prodigal's Prayer

We know this story alright.
We know it not just because we've heard it read and told
among Christian peoples.
Quite beyond that fact we know this story because
we've lived it ourselves.
Each of us has experienced in our own life what it
is to be God's prodigal children.
Let me give you some examples of the ways we
act like prodigal children.
If my examples don't cover you exactly I hope
you'll fit yourself in!

Example 1

My first example starts on a confirmation day or whatever
day it might have been in your young life that you pledged
a special kind of faithfulness to God.
Most of us have those beautiful child-like days of trust
somewhere in our past.
We pledged eternal loyalty to God.

We promised to walk with him forever.
We vowed we would live as his children.
Nothing would distract us.
I remember two days like that from my own youth.
One was my confirmation day.
I was dressed in a clean white robe.
I was surrounded by others in their white robes.
The church was beautifully decorated.
It was great!
"Don't worry about me God. I'm with you.
This is the way it's *always* going to be."
The other day was at Bible Camp.
I was a few years older.
My white-robed confirmation vows were already in shambles.
I had said, "always God."
As it turned out *always* meant about two weeks!
I *needed* to be at that Bible Camp.
I needed renewal.
I was sitting in the chapel with about twenty other young people.
The pastor said,
"Why don't you remember this time and this place (get a picture of it in your mind) as the time you dedicated your life to God."
I DID!
"This time God, I mean always."
This time always meant about three weeks!
I ran away again.
I always run from God it seems.
I wonder if I'll ever stop.
I run away, I run back, I run away,
I run back.

On my way back I pray:
"I have sinned against heaven and against you.
I am not worthy to be called your child."
But, will God hear my prayer?
Will God hear *our* prayers?

Example 2

That's one example of our prodigality.
Here's another.
We make a solemn promise to be loyal to another person.
It may be a parent, it may be our best friend, it may be our husband or wife.
We pledge faithfulness.
We'll keep our word.
We'll be true to our side of the relationship.
Count on us.
Count on me.
But before anyone can count very far we've broken our promise.
"Don't worry, Mom, I won't do it again." . . . but we do!
"Don't worry good friend, the secrets of your heart are safe with me." . . . but they aren't!
"Don't worry sweetheart. I'll be faithful to you always."
However it is that we've shattered human relationships through our prodigal behavior, we find ourselves coming before God again and again with the prodigal's prayer:
"I have sinned against heaven and before you.
I am not worthy to be called your child."
But will God hear?

Example 3

We all know God's law.

We know in our heart and our conscience what God expects from us.

As Christians we know God's law in a condensed form we call the Ten Commandments:

"You shall have no other gods before me."

"Remember the sabbath day. . . . "

"Don't kill." (Jesus said, " . . . every one who is angry with his brother shall be liable to judgment" Matt. 5:22.)

"Don't commit adultery." (Jesus said, " . . . everyone who looks at another lustfully has already committed adultery in one's heart" Matt. 5:28.)

"Don't steal."

"Don't covet."

All that is *part* of God's law.

I think most of us know instinctively that the God behind the Law is always a God who makes *conditional promises* with us.

The conditional promise of the law is:

"DO THIS (that's the condition),

AND YOU WILL LIVE (that's the promise)."

"Do this and you will live."

That's simple enough.

"Do this and you shall be God's child eternally!"

Wonderful!

There's just one catch.

WE DON'T DO IT.

We don't keep God's laws and conditions.

None of us has.

We are prodigals.

We've gone our own way.

We deserve to die.

On the way to our dying we cry out the prodigal's prayer:

"I have sinned against heaven and before you. I am not worthy to be called your child."

Let me have some space in your kingdom, God.

Have mercy upon me.

That's our prayer.

That's the nearly universal prayer of all humanity, of all prodigals.

BUT, will God,

does God,

hear?

Part Two: The Word of the Father

We recognize the prodigal son in this story.

He acts the way we act.

He is all too familiar to all of us.

But the prodigal son is not the only character in this story.

The story is also about a father and a brother.

Let's turn our attention to the father.

It's clear, I think, that if the prodigal son in this story acts like we act, then the father acts like God acts.

The prodigal had his prayer of confession ready:

"I have sinned against heaven and before you."

Would the father hear?

Would he show mercy?

Would he be gracious?

Would he?

AND HOW!

He hardly gave his son a chance to get the words out of his mouth.

The father saw him at a distance,

and he ran out,

and he said:

"Bring quickly the best robe, and put it on him; and put a ring on his hand, and shoes on his feet."

Restore him to full sonship!

For he was dead, and is alive again.

He was lost, but now he's found.

We've broken our vows of faithfulness to God so many, many times.

The prodigal's prayer is on our lips.

But will God hear?

We've shattered the promises we've made to other people.

The prodigal's prayer is on our lips.

But will God hear?

We have broken God's laws of life time and again.

The prodigal's prayer is on our lips.

But will God hear?

Will God hear? Yes!

He hears and the words from this text become his words addressed to you and me; to each of us:

Bring quickly!—the best robe.

Bring quickly!—the ring.

Bring quickly!—shoes for their feet.[1]

Get your family clothes on.

Today you are my child.

You were dead, now you are alive.

You were lost, now you are found.

Powerful words these.

Words of welcome and healing.

What I would like to have you do now is to hear them again as you speak them to each other.

Would you all stand up, please.

Everyone face the center.

You people on my left are the prodigals.

You on the right will speak God's words.

Left side, ready, repeat after me:

I have sinned against heaven,

and before you.

I am not worthy

to be called God's child.

Right side, you speak the father's word, and that's God's word, back to them.

Repeat after me:

Bring quickly the best robe

and the ring

and the shoes.

You were dead,

now you are alive.

You were lost,

now you are found.

(Repeat the process with the right side speaking the prodigal's part.)

You can be seated.

There's only one piece of a verse left in this story before we come to the older brother's role.

That verse says, "And they began to make merry."

In other words, they had a party.

There was a celebration!

Is it any wonder?

A father had his son back.

That's celebrating time.

The God and Father of Our Lord Jesus Christ has you and me back as his children.

That's celebrating time, too.

So let's celebrate.[2]

Let's have a feast!

As a matter of fact, the festal table is already set.

Look. The bread is here.

So is the wine.

The table is set and you're all welcome to come.

You're dressed for the party.

Welcome to the table where God embraces prodigals.

His words for you here are a little bit different from the words we've heard from today's text.

They're different words—but the reality of the welcome is the same.

"This is my body. It is given for you."

"This is my blood. It is shed for you."

"You were dead, now you are alive."

"You were lost, now you are found."

Amen.

Notes

1. These articles (robe, ring and shoes) could have been brought to the front of the sanctuary and put in a place where all could see them. At this point in the sermon they may be referred to with a gesture of the hand or in some other manner.
2. It is important that this sermon lead to some form of "doing celebration" that is appropriate in your tradition. It might be a hymn, prayers or some form of sharing. I have concluded the sermon leading to the eucharistic celebration fitting in my church's tradition.

The second sermon that I have chosen to repre-sent the proclamatory type is based on a sermon I preached at the ordination service of two of my for-mer seminary students. I thought it would be an ap-propriate sermon to illustrate this type because most of the people reading this book will have had their own ordination day. An ordination sermon, there-fore, may serve as an occasion for a living word of God from the Gospel of Matthew to address you to-day in the midst of your present struggles as a pas-tor in God's church. The sermon is clearly directed at the ministry of those about to serve as ordained clergy in the Lutheran theological tradition. I trust that pastors in other theological traditions may be able to apply its "Matthew-word" to their own pas-toral life and mission.

Jesus Announces a Word of Rest

Matthew 11:28-30

Introduction

An ordination day is always a special day for me.

It's a day of solemnity and a day of joy.

It's an occasion that brings many fond memories of the days that have preceded it.

It anticipates days yet to be born.

It's a day of beauty:

— the church glistens

— the choirs are decked out in their finest robes

— banners and stoles splash a rainbow of color before our eyes.

Now it is obvious that all this beauty did not get here by accident.

A lot of people have been very busy preparing for this day.

Indeed the day itself is full of busy-ness.

I think that's good.

Let the busy-ness of this day be a token of the many busy, busy

days of pastoral ministry that
wait for you just around the
curtain of this night's fall.

Old Testament Background for the Text

As busy as this day is, however, it is not nearly as busy as
God was in his first week of activity in our world.

He made light where there was darkness.

He made dry land appear in the midst of the watery
chaos.

He sprinkled the heavens with sun, moon and stars.
And so on it went.

Finally, climactically, he created us, man and
woman, male and female, in his own image!

That's a busy week—even for God!

So on the seventh day God rested.

He blessed the seventh day and hallowed it as a day of rest.

"Remember the sabbath day, to keep it holy . . . for in six
days the Lord made heaven and earth, the sea, and all that
is in them, and rested the seventh day. . . ." (Exod. 20:8,
11.)

We know that as the Third Commandment.

Clearly, many generations of Israelites kept that commandment as they keep it today.

"Remember," they were commanded.

They remembered!

They participated with God in a sabbath day
of rest.

Time stood still.

The six days of toil and labor ceased.

We ought to be able to appreciate and
understand the longing that must have

been felt for the sabbath—for a day of rest.

Life is hectic,
life is struggle,
life is conflict,
life is toil.

If only we could participate with God in an island of rest amidst a sea of trouble!

Sabbath rest meant and sabbath rest means peace and truce and stillness and calm.

Israel longed for such a day.

We do too.

As the Old Testament story unfolds another kind of rest comes into view.

This was not a rest that was *remembered*, like the sabbath—

this was a rest that was *promised*.

You remember the story.

The Israelites were slaves in Egypt.

Moses led them out of Egypt, through the sea and into the land of promise.

The land, however, was full of enemies.

Israel had to fight for her right to live in her land of promise.

That was true for much of her history.

In the midst of Israel's fighting and struggles God promised a day of rest that would bring peace from all conflict.

On that day every one would sit under his own vine and under his own fig tree. (1 Kings 4:25.)

That's the typical picture in the Old Testament of a promised rest.

At times the people of Israel thought that promise had been fulfilled.

Generally, however, it was seen as a word of promise.
It was a word of hope.
Israel waited expectantly.
They waited for God to keep his promise and give her rest from all her enemies.

Jesus Enters the Tradition

The Old Testament has a long and hallowed understanding of God's rest.
On the one hand, it was a remembered sabbath rest.
Sabbath rest was peace and truce and stillness and calm in the midst of life's labors and conflicts.
On the other hand, rest was something in the future, something God had promised.
It was rest from the pursuit of the enemy.
In the Matthew text chosen for this ordination day, Jesus enters this twofold tradition concerning rest.
He announces that he is the fulfillment of this tradition.
"Come to me, all who labor and are heavy laden,
I will give you rest."
Come to me, says Jesus, and you will participate in God's sabbath rest.
Come to me, says Jesus, and you will find rest for your soul,
you will find peace,
you will find stillness,
you will find calm.
Come to me, says Jesus, and you will find rest from your enemies.
When we hear that promise we probably

don't think of rest from the Canaanite
enemy.

We think, rather, of the enemies that
threaten our world: temptation, doubt,
despair, and so on.

Finally we think of God's future promised rest.

We think of eternal life.
"Come to me, all who labor and are heavy laden,
I will give you rest."

I will *give* you rest.

The rest that is ours in Jesus is not a rest that we earn
or achieve or deserve.

"I give you rest."

That is Jesus' word.

That's the good news of the gospel.

The Pastoral Vocation as Announcement of Rest

You have chosen this text for your ordination.

You have emblazoned it on a banner and planted it at
the front of the church this afternoon for all of us to see.

Today it becomes your turn to step into this old tradition concerning rest.

Today we ordain you to speak for Jesus,
to proclaim his Word,
to announce to all who will hear you:
"Come to me, all who labor and are heavy
laden,
I will give you rest."

1. Baptism

You will make this announcement on behalf of Jesus in
your ministry every time you baptize a newborn child.

All kinds of parents are going to come to you to have their children baptized.

Some will come out of habit,
some out of faithfulness,
some out of the midst of their own uncertainties.
Some will come to please their families,
some will come to get a "guaranteed ticket for heaven,"
some will come for fear that their child may die.

I know this last fear from twofold personal experience.

My son and I were both baptized on the brink of death. I know what it's like to see my child baptized in a bleak hospital bed, with a tube hanging out of his nose and hope lying dim in the room.

Parents like me and many others will beat a steady parade to your baptismal font.

The cast of characters you will confront there is just that: a cast of characters.

In the midst of that character-filled cast,
standing at the font,
you are to open your arms and announce the word of Jesus to all who come:

"Come to me, all who labor and are heavy laden,
I will give you rest."

2. The Lord's Supper

You will make this announcement on behalf of Jesus to many of the same cast of characters as you preside at the Lord's Supper.

Some people will come to that table out of sheer habit,
some out of faithfulness,

some in the midst of their own uncertainties.

Alongside of them will march a whole host of the world's unworthy citizens.

Tom and Sue will be there. They're contemplating divorce.

Gertrude, the town gossip, will be there.

She turns loose untrustworthy shock waves wherever she opens her mouth.

George will be there. He just got kicked off the high school football team for drinking.

Sally will be there. She's great with child but has no husband.

Who among this crowd is worthy to eat at this table?

We Lutherans have always been deeply concerned about that.

To eat and drink the body of our Lord in an unworthy manner is to eat and drink judgment upon ourselves (1 Cor. 11:27).

But worthy never meant sinless.

In Luther's catechism it reads: ". . . that person is well prepared and worthy who believes these words, *given and shed for you for the remission of sins*."

You are not presiding over a meal for the so-called saints.

The Lord's table is set for sinners.

It is set for all who will hear Christ's words of promise and believe them.

In the midst of a sinful humanity, preside over that table with graciousness.

Try to fling your arms as wide open as Jesus does his when you say:

> "Come to me all who labor and are
> heavy laden,
> I will give you rest."

3. Preaching

You will make this announcement on behalf of Jesus as you stand in the pulpit Sunday after Sunday.

You are called upon to open the Scriptures for today's people.

That's an awesome task.

And yet, it's a very simple task.

It's simple because the people in your pews are so much like the people in the biblical text itself! Your congregations will be filled with biblical types of people.

Eve will be in every pew.

Eve-like people are all those who wish to "be like god," who wish to play god.

That's one of our basic ways of talking about sin: Pride.

Adam will be there, too.

He'll be just as well represented as Eve.

Adam-like people run away from God's presence and fill the air with their excuses about their inability to be what they ought to be.

That's another basic way we have of talking about sin:

it's the failure to take responsibility for our own lives.

Cain may be there.

He doesn't want to be his brother's keeper.

"Look out for yourself first."

That's his motto.

Job may be there.

He complains a lot.

He complains about everything that happens in his life.

Peter may be there, too.

He's always committing blunders,

always trying to do things his own way.

Martha will show up occasionally.

Usually she is just too busy working in the kitchen to be able to get away.

Judas might even show up.

You know, the one who seeks to undermine and betray your ministry among the people of God.

From your lonely perch in the pulpit you will look out on all of these "biblical types" of people.

And what will you say to them?

"Come to me all who labor and are heavy laden,

I will give you rest."

Conclusion

The word you are to proclaim is clear.

The gospel treasure is yours to announce to all.

"But we have this treasure in earthen vessels. . . ." (2 Cor. 4:7.)

Earthen indeed!

There are some difficult and trying times ahead of you in ministry.

There will be times when you want to throw in the towel.

There will be times when you wonder if anyone cares.

There will be times when you are going to

be bone-weary from the task that lies before you.

I hope you will take this lovely banner you have placed in the front of the church this afternoon along with you.

Hang it in a place where you will be sure to see it from time to time.

Many days are coming when you will need the reminder that Jesus' words are also words for you.

Bone-weary you will need to see and hear this word of Jesus addressed new and afresh to you:

"Come to me all who labor and are heavy laden,
I will give you rest."

Amen.

5

STORY PREACHING

THE THIRD TYPE OF PREACHING could carry a number of titles. I have chosen to call it Story Preaching. I make this choice because *story* captures the breadth of what I wish to communicate and does so in simple terminology. I use the word *story* to mean narration. I never use it in the negative sense (it was *only* a story).

Another possible title for this type would be "preaching as fairy tale." That's the way Frederick Buechner goes about describing the task of communicating the gospel in his wonderfully inventive and fascinating book, *Telling the Truth.*[1] Perhaps it is only in the world of fairy tales—a world we have all inhabited at one time or another, a world full of darkness, danger, and ambiguity, a world where things are not what they seem as marvelous transformations take place, a world that evokes new adventures and new possibilities, a world where good finally wins the day in a triumph of marvelous surprise—that the wonder and surprise and ambiguity and transforming power and final triumph of the gospel of Jesus Christ can be set forth.

With his fabulous tale to proclaim, the preacher is called in his turn to stand up in his pulpit as fabulist extraordinary, to tell the truth of the Gospel in its highest and wildest and holiest sense.[2]

But who among us dares to soar into such a madcap world in order that the "folly of what we preach" (1 Cor. 1:21) might be heard in such a way that listener's worlds are turned upside down? This gospel business is madness! Who will believe it? Who will believe this mad-fool God who through his incarnate Son (that's enough foolishness already!) welcomes tax collectors and sinners and prostitutes and other assorted human losers into his marvelous and graceful kingdom? Who will dare? The preacher, losing his or her daring, oftimes exchanges

> . . . the fairy-tale truth that is too good to be true for a truth that instead of drowning out all the other truths the world is loud with is in some kind of harmony with them. He secularizes and makes rational. He adapts and makes relevant. He demythologizes and makes credible. . . . For the sake, as he sees it, of the ones he preaches to, the preacher is apt to preach the Gospel with the high magic taken out, the deep mystery reduced to a manageable size.[3]

People all over the world are proclaiming fairy tales that never come true to people who trust mightily that those tales are believable. Preachers have the highest and holiest of all fairy tales to tell . . . a tale that is (incredibly!) true. So incredible is it, in fact, that few preachers risk the telling. In a world of fascinating tales, mysterious secrets of the earth and exciting vistas of outer space—preaching is boring. That at least is Buechner's fear. We've let the holy mysteries slip through our fingers. Fairy tales are for children, after all. Indeed they are . . . for children of all ages. "Unless you become as a little child. . . ."

Buechner is on to something. Preaching as fairy tale! Why not? I can hear many objections. Fairy tales, after all, don't take us *directly* to the point. They ease us into a world of make-believe where the good news possibilities of the gospel are hinted at in oblique ways. In the world of fairy tale we are not confronted with the gospel. There is no direct encounter that leads us to decision for or against.

Our culture has become accustomed to direct approaches, to confrontations, to encounters. We tell it like it is. Everything is on the table. Encounter groups are sometimes conducted in the nude so that nothing is hidden. Eyeball to eyeball. Straight talk. That is the environment of communication in which we live. The proclamatory preaching we discussed in Chapters 3 and 4 grows naturally out of this communication environment. It is an environment that says in every conceivable way, "Get to the point and get there in the most direct fashion." Fairy tales don't survive in that kind of environment. No story does! Stories take too many side trips. They don't go straight to the point.

I am not proposing fairy-tale as a preaching type. My proposal is for Story Preaching. I think story preaching has become possible in our culture today precisely because the communication environment we have been describing has changed. People have grown weary of constant eyeball to eyeball confrontation and direct encounters. The signs that this is the case, the signs that the communication environment in which we live has altered, are increasingly visible. Stories have a future among us. Let me just point to some instances that give me the confidence to make this kind of statement.

"Jay O'Callahan has revived the ancient art of storytelling." That was the subtitle of a *Time* magazine article on June 19, 1978. Mr. O'Callahan is, of all things, a storyteller-in-residence for the public schools in Quincy, Framingham, and Brookline, Massachusetts. In this technological age where young people "have seen everything on TV," students will actually skip lunch or gym class to attend O'Callahan's storytelling time. Why? Says O'Callahan, "People are hungry for storytelling because we live in an age preoccupied with technology and science."

The world of the theater presents us with another startling success of the storyteller's art and craft. An English actor by the name of Alec McCowen has had what most people would call unbelievable theatrical success in England and in the United States with a one-man, straightforward recital of the Gospel of Mark. McCowen chose Mark's gospel because it was the easiest of the gospels to *tell aloud*. And that's what McCowen does. He tells it aloud. No lines added. No stage props. No catchy tunes to jazz up the piece. McCowen simply tells the audience the story of Jesus the way he thinks Mark would have told it. Simple oral recitation by a master orator. Audiences have flocked to his performance. They come to hear the story. The presentation is much longer than the average sermon—but no one complains!

The best-selling theologian in the world at the present time is also a consummate storyteller—C. S. Lewis. Some people would argue about calling Lewis a theologian. But such a quarrel misses the point. The point is that Lewis has reached an audience with his "theologizing" which most theologians never penetrate. The masses read the theology of C. S. Lewis. The common people read and are inspired. This is so because people of all ages are touched by his storytelling skill. His best seller in the 1970s was *Mere Christianity*. That work has some of the markings of classic theology. Many of his other best sellers, however, are pure story in form—*The Screwtape Letters, The Great Divorce, The Chronicles of Narnia.*

One of Lewis's closest colleagues has also produced his theology in story form. I am referring to J. R. R. Tolkien, the author of *The Hobbit, The Lord of the Rings,* and *The Silmarillion.* There has been an almost cult-like reverence for Tolkien's stories of Middle Earth. As we shall see later on in this chapter Tolkien, like Lewis, is a self-consciously Christian writer who has used the story form as the vehicle for communicating the gospel as he understands it.

Perhaps we should not be surprised that Christian storytellers of the stature of Lewis and Tolkien have risen out of John Bunyan's England. Bunyan's *Pilgrim's Progress* was for many years the second most widely read book in the English language. It ranked second only to the Bible—a book with stories beyond compare! It is worth noting that responsible scholars have called Bunyan's story of the Christian life the most influential religious book ever composed in the English language. Stories have power!

In our own country the greatest storytelling theologian is probably the Jewish writer Elie Wiesel. In novel after novel Wiesel has tried to make sense out of what it means to be a Jew after Auschwitz by telling stories about the ongoing struggles of life in relationship to and in the context of biblical stories. Wiesel comes by his storytelling art naturally. Through the ages Jewish religious scholars have been asked every conceivable theological question. They have seldom answered these questions directly. The typical answer of the Jewish religious scholar (rabbi) to a good question does not usually begin with words like, "The answer to your question is. . . ." That's the direct approach. More typically his answer will begin, "Let me tell you a story. . . ." That's an indirect approach.

Stories have always been with us. They are an ancient hallowed and extremely effective form of human communication. *So why can't sermons be stories?* That's the question that has haunted me for the past several years. I will illustrate the background of my hauntedness simply. The United States has had a racial problem with a long and tortuous history. Many books have been written seeking to sensitize our citizenry on this subject. We all have access and perhaps we have all read books about slavery. Well and good. Then one January we sat night after night and watched a story: *Roots.* For many Americans *Roots* was the first event, the first story, that broke into their world with the reality of human hatred and injustice that is the racial problem of America.

I've given a good deal of thought to the difference in impact between reading about slavery and watching a powerful story *(Roots).* A book about slavery gives me all the data and facts and information that I need. *Roots* moved me. It moved all kinds of people. Many viewers reported that at the conclusion of the final episode their children went running off through the house shouting to any and all who would listen, "They're free! They're free!"

Why can't preaching be like that? Why can't preaching be more like *Roots* in its power and impact and less like a cold, unemotional book? I'm afraid the reverse is true. Most of our preaching, didactic in character, imparts all of the information, data and facts. But no one is moved. Very few go off shouting, "I'm free! I'm free!" Couldn't we learn to tell stories in such a way that people's lives would be changed? Changed lives, transformed people—that's what the gospel is all about. Couldn't the storytellers' art aid us in our preaching task? That is the question that lies at the heart of this chapter. I hope I can answer it affirmatively to your satisfaction and to mine.

Story in Theological and Biblical Studies

From 1964-1973 Martin Marty and Dean Peerman edited ten volumes of *new theology* with the intention of monitoring yearly what was new in the field of theology. Had there been an eleventh volume, Marty has said, it would have been on "Story and Theology." The phenomenon of story has returned not only as a culturally viable mode of communication but also as a viable theological form. People's stories have become the focus of theological investigation both in the form of autobiographies (John Dunne, *A Search for God in Time and Memory*) and biographies (James McLendon, *Biography as Theology*). Augustine's *Confessions* have taken on new importance. College and seminary courses in these areas have abounded. The patron saints of early twentieth century theology have returned in any number of biographical forms.

A number of quality books have appeared in the past decade which take the story form seriously for the theological enterprise.[4] The return of story to the world of theology represents a definite and radical shift in theological sensibilities in the last quarter of the twentieth century. Western theology has been dominated for two centuries by the thought world of the Enlightenment.

> Cartesian man had the audacity to think thoughts . . . which, if they were practicable, would have at one and the same time enabled and forced him to live entirely without stories. By mastering nature, industrializing work, rebelling politically, taming the unconscious, identifying man as but another of the evolving forms of life, an objectifying consciousness tried to leave behind modes

of perception which are the fertile soil from which stories arise. . . . It was indeed, as Stephen Crites so pungently observed, a story to end all stories.[5]

What fascinates Wiggins and what fascinates me is the fact that the story to end all stories, i.e. the Enlightenment, has suddenly failed. Stories are everywhere! The plot to end all stories can now be seen for what it is: the story of the *plot* to end all stories! Our culture has taken a fancy to storytelling once again. Impulses of a romantic (as in Romanticism) nature have pushed through the arid Enlightenment clay. Even theologians are telling stories again. Demythologization (part of the plot to end all stories) has lost its iron grip on the Western theological mind. Bultmann's demything has given way to Tolkien's myth-making. That's a wondrously long journey!

Biblical studies have also given renewed attention to the stories and story forms of the Bible. The probing work here was done by Amos Wilder in 1964 in a little noticed (at the time) book entitled *Early Christian Rhetoric: The Language of the Gospel*. It is a study of the literary forms of the early church. Wilder's assumption is that there is a symmetry between *what* the early Christians wished to say about Jesus and *how* they chose to say it. A new message, the gospel of Jesus Christ, demanded new forms of communication. The gospels are a new kind of literature. They are literature based on oral communication. When gospels and other documents were written down for posterity they retained the personal, firsthand reporting of the oral tradition. Three particular speech forms appear in the earliest tradition of gospel communication: dialog, story, and poetry.

> The word of God found its appropriate vehicles both in the sense of images and of forms. Within limits one can say that to this very day and always Christianity will

most characteristically communicate itself at least in these three modes: the drama, the narrative, the poem—just as it will always be bound in some degree to its primordial symbols, no matter how much the world may change. In a double sense Father Thornton's statement holds true: "The contents of the revelation are mysteriously inseparable from the forms in which they are conveyed." [6]

The implications of Wilder's work are clear. If we wish to communicate the gospel we must use dialog, story, and poetry. They are the indispensable forms for communicating the gospel. The message of the gospel demands these forms if it is to be effectively communicated. We may find other useful forms as well but Wilder says that to dispense totally with these forms is to dispense with the gospel itself. Form and content cannot easily be divorced.

Biblical scholarship has followed Wilder's lead. Much greater attention has been paid in recent years to the literary form of biblical texts. Structuralism, a new tool of biblical study, has concerned itself with relating the structures of biblical stories to the structures of human life and thought. However, structuralism as a biblical discipline seems to me to have certain deficiencies. Its strength is assuredly its interest in the holistic character, the wider context, of biblical stories. We have survived every kind of exegesis that has sought to analyze and shred biblical stories into their smallest fragments. To be enabled to hear the stories as stories in their canonical context again is very helpful.

Nowhere in biblical studies has the interest in story been more evident than in the new work being done in parable studies. The work of Dan Otto Via, Jr., John Dominic Crossan and many others has opened up new horizons in understanding the parables of Jesus. We will

look at a few of the important findings of this work later
on in this chapter as we seek to connect new insights into
parables with the task of preaching in story form.

The Psychology of Consciousness [7]

We have been describing some of the facts of our cultural situation. We live in a time when an emphasis on
direct, eyeball to eyeball communication is being supple-
mented by the more indirect communicative style of storytelling. We have noted instances of this supplementation
in education, in the arts and in theological and biblical
studies. Humanity, it seems, cannot live by direct, logical, rational, orderly discourse alone. Our biological construction, the way our brains function, won't allow it.
That is the argument that is increasingly heard as the
result of new studies on the human brain. Robert Ornstein's book, *The Psychology of Consciousness* is a useful
summary of these findings.

Ornstein notes that Roger Bacon had told us 700 years
ago that there are two modes of knowing: argument and
experience.

> One mode is verbal and rational, sequential in operation,
> orderly; the other is intuitive, tacit, diffuse in operation,
> less logical and neat, a mode we often devalue, culturally,
> personally, and even physiologically.[8]

Ornstein tries to get these two modes of knowing in balance and perspective again. This is important, says Ornstein, because everyone has the capability of learning in
each of these modes. We have linear, rational modes of
perception and we have nonrational and intuitive modes
of perception. In some people one of these modes may be
dominant. Some have argued that women may "know"
more by intuition; men by rational deduction. The truth is

probably that each of us has our own unique combination of these modes of perception.

The intriguing thing about these studies is that our perceptual modalities may have a biological base in the construction of the brain. One way this was discovered was in patients who had surgical operations to separate the two hemispheres of the brain.

For example, when a blindfolded patient was given a piece of chalk in his right hand, he could name what it was. (Verbal thought.) When the chalk was placed in a patient's left hand, he was unable to give its proper name but could act out how to use it. The patient had an overall understanding of the object, a "wholistic" (or "holistic") view of the whole object—he just couldn't think of its name until it was put into his right hand.[9]

The difference between the left and right sides of the body may provide a key to open our understanding of the psychological and physiological mechanisms of the two major modes of consciousness. The cerebral cortex of the brain is divided into two hemispheres, joined by a large bundle of interconnecting fibers called the "corpus callosum." The left side of the body is mainly controlled by the right side of the cortex, and the right side of the body by the left side of the cortex. . . . The left hemisphere . . . is predominantly involved with analytic, logical thinking, especially in verbal and mathematical functions. Its mode of operation is primarily linear. This hemisphere seems to process information sequentially . . . the right hemisphere . . . seems specialized for holistic mentation. Its language ability is quite limited. This hemisphere is primarily responsible for our orientation in space, artistic endeavor, crafts, body image, recognition of faces. . . . If the left hemisphere can be termed predominantly analytic and sequential in its operation, then the right hemisphere is more holistic and relational, and more simultaneous in its mode of operation.[10]

Many other illustrations and examples of the left brain (which controls our rational, logical, sequential thought processes) and right brain (which controls our intuitive, holistic, imagistic thought processes) phenomenon could be given. I am more interested in the implications of this left brain/right brain hypothesis than in supplying technical detail and supportive documentation. The detail and documentation is available to any who wish to pursue the subject.

Let's just suppose that this description of human perception is true. The implications for the art of preaching are numerous. Some of those implications are as follows:

1. Didactic and proclamatory preaching will probably communicate most clearly to those hearers whose dominant mode of perception is controlled by the left hemisphere of the brain.

2. Neither didactic nor proclamatory preaching will communicate clearly to those hearers whose dominant mode of perception is controlled by the right hemisphere of the brain.

3. If there is any truth at all to the left brain/right brain hypothesis (and most of us sense instinctively that there are some people who grasp things logically and some people who grasp things by intuition!) then we have a responsibility as preachers of the gospel to develop types of preaching, that communicate with both modes of perception. Story preaching is my suggestion for fulfilling this responsibility in relation to the right hemisphere of the brain.

My interest in story preaching is not by any means limited to theories of the brain. As a matter of fact I discovered the left brain/right brain hypothesis after I had begun to study the story form. I don't wish to overlook this new evidence but neither do I wish to make this evidence into a kind of scientific theory for story preaching.

Stories are universally human modes of communication. There has never been a time in human history when stories have not been shared among human beings as a way of coming to terms with life in time and space. Stories are popular among us today. The Bible is essentially a story book. Preaching that is faithful to the Bible and faithful to shared human history and experience will find room for the storytellers art. Communicating the gospel via the medium of storytelling is not a luxury that we might choose to adopt. Storytelling and gospel-telling are inextricably wrapped up with one another. That was the point Amos Wilder was making. It is time now to pursue the story type in more detail.

Characteristics of Story Preaching

1. *The biblical text is treated as a particular configuration of literary form* (how the message is communicated) *and content* (what the message is) *which has serious implications for our contemporary recasting of the text.*

We have alluded earlier to Amos Wilder's point that biblical form and content (the *how* and the *what* of the text) cannot easily be separated from each other. He finds, however, that the history of biblical study is primarily a history of the divorce of form from content. People who have been interested in the "Bible as literature" are quite often uninterested in the content or kerygma of the biblical text. An existential hermeneutic (the hermeneutics of Fuchs, Ebeling, Bultmann) often errs at the other end of the spectrum by separating out the content from the biblical literary form.

Wilder would be critical of proclamatory preaching to the extent that it lifts content out of its biblical literary moorings. Wilder aims his critical sights on Bulmann or anyone else who treats biblical images and metaphors as myths from which we need to extract the real meaning or kerygma. We cannot know the so-called meaning of the text apart from the images and metaphors in which it is communicated to us. The literary form of the text, its images, symbols and metaphors, cannot be separated from the kerygma of the text.

> What the early Christian faith meant, therefore, can only be grasped as we attend to its plastic language, giving full heed to what it meant in its original setting. . . . These images mean what they meant to the early witnesses in all their rich connotations. Our congenital modern demand that such language be rationalized must be resisted. . . . We thus vindicate the intrinsic importance of the early Christian rhetoric in its aspects of imagery. . . . We appropriate the myth and symbol of the New Testament by opening ourselves to its wisdom in the same order of response with which we encounter art or read poetry. Though this order of knowing is closer to that of ancient spell or visionary realization, or the world-making of the child, yet it is, for this very reason, a total and immediate kind of knowing and one that involves us totally.[11]

Without realizing it Wilder here describes a way of knowing that is almost identical to the perceptual mode of knowing characteristic of the so-called right hemisphere of the brain!

My first brush with Wilder put me in such a foreign world that I hardly knew what to do. Most biblical preachers have become experts at wrangling the content out of the form of the text. Creation, fall, the rise of the monarchy in Israel, the role of suffering (Job), the reluctance of Israel and all people to fulfill their missionary vocation (Jonah), redemption, crucifixion, resurrection, the history of the early church are all told in the biblical text in some kind of story form. We get the point of the story and construct a sermon around that point.

Amos Wilder says that although that may be a legitimate homiletical practice on occasion we ought to realize that when we extract points and meanings from biblical stories we are doing violence to the marriage of literary form and content that is the total configuration of the biblical text. (Wilder's thesis concerning form and content is supported by an increasing number of biblical scholars.) If the text "makes its point" in story form then we ought to seriously consider constructing a sermon that is faithful to the content and the form of the biblical text. Let us also tell a story of the fall, let us tell a story regarding suffering, let us tell a story about dying and rising with Christ, etc.

The biblical writers very often communicate with us through stories. Why should we de-story these stories in our sermons and simply pass on the point of the story to our listeners? Why should we rip the content out of the form as our normal homiletical process? If the story (or whatever literary form the text may take) is of no matter why didn't the biblical writer just tell us the point in the first place? Why didn't the author of Genesis 2-3 just tell us what sin is? Why did he or she tell a story? And if that biblical author carefully constructed a "sin story" why do we always feel compelled to improve on the story by preaching on the point?

What I am getting at under this first point is the fact that our style of exegesis for preaching may have to undergo some radical shifts. Exegesis has been directed primarily at the question of content. A holistic exegesis must be directed at both form and content. It is not enough to get the meaning *out of* the text and into the sermon. We must pay attention to the total configuration of textual form/content. How can the biblical images that come to us in this textual union of form and content be imaginatively recast in our sermons? Story preaching comes to life in the process of imaginative recasting. That's what preaching as storytelling is all about. It is a recasting of textual imagery. The text in its totality gives rise to certain images. The sermon may present these images in a recast union of form/content that is faithful to the biblical text. The sermon, in that case, is interested not only in the content but also in the form of the text. The exegetical question is, "How can this total textual configuration of form and content be recast?" Oftentimes that recasting will take a story form!

Think, just for a moment, of the story of Jonah. The point of what happens in that story is inseparable from the story itself. Preaching need not simply re-tell the story—although we probably could do just that in some cases. We can, however, create and tell our own stories which elicit responses in the hearer similar to the responses to the original story. What is lost to our hearers so often is the context in which this Jonah-story *spoke for itself*. But surely we can tell a story in our own context that speaks for itself and that speaks the story of Jonah anew in our time. That's imaginative recasting. That's preaching as storytelling. And we can do that not only with the story of Jonah but with many biblical texts as we seek to be faithful to the biblical text: content *and* form.

2. *The story is the preaching itself.*

James Reese offers the following quotation from Flannery O'Connor on the nature of her stories:

People have a habit of saying, "What is the theme of your story?" and they expect you to give them a statement: "The theme of my story is the economic pressure of the machine on the middle class"—or some such absurdity. And when they've got a statement like that, they go off happy and feel it is no longer necessary to read the story.[12]

This quotation from Flannery O'Connor says in its own way that, "the story is the preaching itself." She writes her stories, dramatists write their plays, novelists write their novels and movie makers produce their movies as a way of communicating truth as they see it. That at least is the purpose behind the best of the arts. At the end of a novel the novelist does not tell us, "Now the point of this novel is. . . . " At the end of a play the playwright does not come out and say, "Now the meaning of my play was. . . . " At the end of a provocative film the film-maker does not append an epilog saying, "What I was trying to get at was. . . ." The story, the novel, the play, the film, the painting etc. is the preaching itself. In its most developed form a story sermon is also the preaching itself!

When I am talking about story preaching, therefore, *I am not talking about using stories in order to illustrate points!* In his work on the parables of Jesus, John Dominic Crossan distinguishes between several different kinds and uses of metaphors. First a definition of a metaphor:

I. A. Richards says, "in the simplest formulation, when we use a metaphor we have two thoughts of different things active together and supported by a single word, or phrase, whose meaning is a resultant of their interaction." [13]

This juxtaposing of two different thoughts which is the metaphor is thought by most people, says Crossan, to be a *dispensable* feature of language and communication.

Some people are convinced that metaphors only confuse the issue. Who understands poets anyway? Dispense with them. Others see metaphors as ornaments of speech. Ornaments are dispensable. Take the ornaments off a Christmas tree and you still have a Christmas tree. Take the metaphorical ornaments out of language usage and you still have meaningful language.

For those who will keep metaphor as part of language usage there are *metaphors of illustration* and *metaphors of participation.* A metaphor of illustration, says Crossan, is dispensable once people have gotten the point you wished to illustrate. Metaphors of illustration are the category in which most sermon illustrations fit. We use some sort of metaphor in order to illustrate our point but once the hearers have gotten the point they have graduated from illustration to information. Having the information fully within their grasp they may dispense with the metaphor.

Metaphors of participation differ from all of the above-mentioned usages of metaphor because they are *indispensable!*

> . . . metaphor can also articulate a referent so new or so alien to consciousness that this referent can only be grasped within the metaphor itself. . . . When a metaphor contains a radically new vision of world it gives absolutely no information until after the hearer has entered into it and experienced it from inside itself.[14]

Crossan is convinced that this latter usage of metaphor, the indispensable metaphor of participation, is the primary way the Bible and Jesus use metaphor. The metaphor is the preaching itself.

Stories are extended metaphors. The use of stories in preaching can certainly be used for illustrative purposes. In that case the story is dispensed with once the point is communicated. I want to hold out for the possibility, however, that story preaching may be a metaphor of participation. The story is itself the preaching. At the end of the story the preacher is not required to come "on stage" and tell the congregation, "Now the point of this story was. . . . " I am convinced that if our people get the point (so to speak) of a novel, a play, a movie, etc. then they can be enabled to get the point of a story sermon without the preacher's explanatory efforts.

My own understanding of this possibility owes its greatest debt to the recent work in biblical studies on the parables of Jesus. Authors coming from a variety of angles have reached an amazing consensus of opinion on the nature of parables as *metaphors of participation*. The history of parable interpretation in the life of the church was dominated for many centuries by an allegorical interpretation. An allegorical interpretation seeks to find a corresponding point of reference for each detail of the parable. Allegory assumes that the reader or hearer (in this case of parable) *already knows* all the information being communicated. We simply need to de-code the allegory to find the points to which it corresponds.

Adolf Julicher challenged the allegorical interpretation of parables. He insisted that the parables made only one point, not several. In trying to understand the parables, Julicher said, we need to catch the whole or single impression which a particular parable might have made on its listeners. Under the influence of Julicher's work preaching on the parables concentrated on the single impression or point of the parable. That impression or point became the heart of the sermon. The parable itself was *dispensable* once the point was discovered. Preaching concentrated on the *content* and left the parabolic *form* behind!

The growing consensus in parable studies is that parables are indeed metaphors of participation and that the metaphorical form of the parable ought not be separated from its content.[15]

> It is this revelatory character of Jesus' parables which is to be stressed . . . in the metaphor we have an image with a certain shock to the imagination which directly conveys visions of what is signified.

> In the parables we have action-images. . . . Now we know that a true metaphor or symbol is more than a sign, it is a bearer of the reality to which it refers. The hearer not only learns about the reality, he participates in it. He is invaded by it. Here lies the power and fatefulness of art. Jesus' speech had the character not of instruction and ideas but of compelling imagination, of spell, of mythical shock and transformation. Not just in an aesthetic sense but in the service of the Gospel.[16]

Dan Otto Via, Jr. argues that parables are aesthetic objects and that they are autotelic, that is, they are self-contained works of art which do not point beyond themselves.

> Aesthetic experience is a particular and unique type of experience . . . it is the experience of intransitive, non-referential, or rapt *attention* to an object which is capable of evoking that kind of experience. In non-aesthetic modes of experience attention is transitive; that is, it is referred beyond the object of concern to other objects and meanings . . . when language is used aesthetically, the form . . . is centripetally organized so that all of the parts tightly cohere with each other. If the artistic work is such a self-contained (i.e. *autotelic*) world of new word combinations, then the belief that it could be successfully rendered into other words or paraphrased can only be labeled heresy.[17]

> Their (the rabbis) stories are didactic figures, those of Jesus are poetic metaphors; theirs are subservient to the

teaching situations, those of Jesus are subservient only to the experienced revelation which seeks to articulate its presence in, by, and through them.

This distinction has been pointed out already by Gunther Bornkamm: "The rabbis also relate parables in abundance, to clarify a point in their teaching. . . . That is just what they are not in the mouth of Jesus. . . . Here the parables are the preaching itself and are not merely serving the purpose of a lesson which is quite independent of them." One might summarize the entire purpose of the present book by stating that it seeks to render explicit all that is contained in that final phrase, "the parables are the preaching itself," especially in the light of the parallel assertion of Ezra Pound, cited in this book's epigraph, that, "the image is itself the speech." [18]

The story is the preaching itself. That is my translation into the art of homiletics of Bornkamm's dictum regarding the parables of Jesus: "the parables are the preaching itself." I am convinced that preaching can be "parabolic" in just that sense. Preaching in story form can be revelatory in and through the medium of the story. It need not point somewhere else. It can be autotelic. It can create an arena in the imagination wherein the listener is caught up and transformed or shocked or good-newsed or whatever. The hearer goes away from the story (sermon) knowing what the story communicated without the preacher's explanation, "Now the point of the story is. . . ." Flannery O'Connor is right. If they know the point they can do without our (story) sermon!

There will be examples of story preaching in Chapter 6. You will see that I adhere to this point that the story is the preaching itself in varying degrees. Some stories require additional (from little to much) explanation. Our congregations are simply not prepared to be plunged immediately into story sermons as ends in themselves! Explanation and story need not be juxtaposed to each other as total opposites. Still I would hold out for the possibility that with proper enabling on the part of the preacher all explanations could be dropped. The story can be the preaching itself!

3. *The aim of the sermon is the participation and involvement of the listener in the gospel story.*

> And the Lord sent Nathan to David. He came to him, and said to him, "There were two men in a certain city, the one rich and the other poor. The rich man had very many flocks and herds; but the poor man had nothing but one little ewe lamb, which he had bought. And he brought it up, and it grew up with him and with his children; it used to eat of his morsel, and drink from his cup, and lie in his bosom, and it was like a daughter to him. Now there came a traveler to the rich man, and he was unwilling to take one of his flock or herd to prepare for the wayfarer who had come to him, but he took the poor man's lamb, and prepared it for the man who had come to him." Then David's anger was greatly kindled against the man; and he said to Nathan, "As the Lord lives, the man who has done this deserves to die." . . . Nathan said to David, "You are the man."—Samuel 12:1-7.

Nathan's famous parable to David illustrates nearly every characteristic of story preaching. I use it here particularly to illustrate the power of story to involve the hearer, to elicit participation. Nathan had recast the situation of David's life in his little story. In this form David failed to recognize himself. He couldn't wait to jump into the story. "He deserves to die!", David shouted. He was so involved in the story that he provided the story's ending. Nathan's story went part way; David finished it. David participated in the completion of the story. He pronounced judgment on himself! Participation is one of the foremost aims of story preaching. It ought to involve the hearer to such an extent that the hearer finishes the story. The hearer supplies the ending. The hearer applies the story to his or her own life making the application a personal one.

This was illustrated beautifully for me several years ago when a professor of homiletics and I did a workshop on story preaching for a large group of pastors and selected laypersons. We had each preached a story sermon. Two responses to our homiletical efforts stand out in my mind. Both indicated that our "sermon" was somehow not the end of the matter. A pastor said, "It seems to me that you have only preached half of the sermon." A laywoman said, "When you stopped, I didn't." We couldn't have planted a better answer! She got caught up in the sermon-story. She was involved. Like David, she had to supply her own ending to the story. She had talked to a number of other people seeking for the clues that would put it all together for her. She participated in those sermons! In the language of John Dominic Crossan, the sermon had created for her a metaphor of participation.

In a famous essay, "On Fairy-Stories," J. R. R. Tolkien talks about the experience/involvement/participation of the reader in the story under the rubric of *eucatastrophe*. Tolkien writes his fairy stories *(The Hobbit, The Lord of the Rings, The Silmarillion)* as a self-conscious expression of his Christian faith. The eucatastrophic tale is, for Tolkien, the true form of fairy tales and a viable form for communicating the joy of the Christian faith. Tolkien's fairy tales are not to be read as allegory. Tolkien, in fact, finds himself at some odds with his friend C. S. Lewis on this issue. He feels that Lewis writes allegory when he writes his fictive pieces. Allegory, as we have noted earlier, sets the reader busy in the decoding process. When Lewis writes x, therefore, we see that he means y; when he writes a he means c etc. (When Lewis writes of Aslan the

Lion in the *Chronicles of Narnia,* for example, every reader immediately decodes that and knows he is really talking about Jesus.)

Not so with Tolkien. He intends no allegories whatsoever. The make-believe world he worked so hard to create, complete with maps and languages, is just that: a make-believe world. Tolkien wants his reader to participate in that make-believe world and experience there the *good turn* (good news) which is the gospel experience:

> The consolation of fairy-stories, the joy of the happy ending: or more correctly of the good catastrophe, the sudden joyous "turn" (for there is no true end to any fairy-tale): this joy which is one of the things which fairy-stories can produce supremely well, is not essentially "escapist," nor "fugitive." In its fairy-tale—or other world—setting, it is a sudden and miraculous grace: never to be counted on to recur. It does not deny the existence of *dyscatastrophe,* of sorrow and failure: the possibility of these is necessary to the joy of deliverance; it denies (in the face of much evidence, if you will) universal final defeat and in so far is *evangelium,* giving a fleeting glimpse of Joy, Joy beyond the walls of the world, poignant as grief.

> It is the mark of a good fairy-story, of the higher or more complete kind, that however wild its events, however fantastic or terrible the adventures, it can give to child or man that hears it, when the "turn" comes, a catch of the breath, a beat and lifting of the heart. . . . [19]

Tolkien wishes his reader to experience a "good turn" (i.e. *eucatastrophe)* in the reading of his stories. Tolkien understands that "good-turn-experience" to be an experience of the gospel, the *evangelium.* The Gospels, he says, contain the fairy story which embraces the essence of all fairy stories.

> The Birth of Christ is the eucatastrophe of Man's history.

> The Resurrection is the eucatastrophe of the story of the Incarnation. This story begins and ends in joy.[20]

Eucatastrophic preaching, therefore, would be story preaching which invites the hearer into the world of the imagination in order that *within the context of that world* the hearer might participate in the "good-turn-experience" which is the gospel. We know how involved we can get in stories. We laugh. We cry. We hope. We wonder. The gospel of our Lord Jesus Christ creates all of these same emotions in us. Tolkien invites us to tell stories that create these emotions leading people to understand that the basic cause of all our joys, hopes and wonders is the too-good-to-be-true-story"; the story of Jesus. I think that can be done.

Story preaching aims to involve the listeners. It may involve them in an experience of seeing themselves for what they really are (cf. Nathan's story to David) or it may involve them in eucatastrophe. We will discuss Fred Craddock's work, *Overhearing the Gospel,* in the next section.

The two basic factors in "overhearing" the gospel, according to Craddock, are *distance* and *participation*.[21] Distance and participation are helpful words to use in order to describe listener involvement in story preaching. Distance creates a certain kind of safety. David was at a distance from his own situation as he listened to Nathan's story. We stand at a distance from our everyday world when we enter Tolkien's fairy-story world. In the safety of this distance we often participate deeply in the story that is told, hearing things about ourselves, judgments and eucatastrophes, that we might not otherwise be able to hear. *Distance enables participation!*

The aim of story preaching is to create a world in story which is safe enough for people to enter (distance) and powerful enough to involve the hearer in personal participation in words of judgment and grace. The aim of story preaching is *experiential*. God's judgment and grace are more than *ideas* that Christians ought to *understand*. I would hope that story preaching might enable people to experience the judgment and grace of God as they complete the story we have begun and apply it personally to their own lives.

4. *Stories function in the indirect mode of communication*. "Tell all the truth, but tell it slant. . . ." —Emily Dickinson.

The above mentioned work of Fred Craddock is a discussion of direct and indirect modes of communication via a discussion of the usages of these modes by the nineteenth century Danish theologian, Søren Kierkegaard. In actuality the entire book is meditation by Craddock on a single quotation from Kierkegaard:

> There is no lack of information in a Christian land; something else is lacking, and this is something which the one man cannot directly communicate to the other.[22]

If conditions are such that the gospel cannot be *directly* communicated to people, then we must search, said Kierkegaard, for *indirect* methods of communicating the good news. Kierkegaard's definitions of these two modes is as follows according to Craddock:

> He regarded direct as the mode for transferring information and totally appropriate to the fields of history, science, and related disciplines. The indirect is the mode for eliciting capability and action from within the listener, a transaction that does not occur by giving the hearer some information.[23]

Kierkegaard himself used the two modes simultaneously, the indirect mode being used as his *primary* style.

Kierkegaard gave several reasons for not using the direct mode of communication as his *primary* method:

1. It is not appropriate to the nature of the Christian faith. God revealed himself to us by hiding himself (that is, indirectly!) in Jesus of Nazareth.

2. It is not information that is lacking. People have more than enough information about the Christian faith. This information, however, must be inwardly appropriated; there needs to be an inward realization of what all this "outward information" means. This realization and appropriation can only be elicited by indirection.

3. The goal of inward appropriation of the gospel by the reader/listener cannot be achieved by "direct thundering" at people. Such thundering is counterproductive! Respect for the solitude of each person's appropriation of the Christian faith can only be achieved by indirection.[24]

Indirect communication is not universally applicable to Christian communication, however. Indirect communication operates on the premise that what is already in the hearer's consciousness is brought to further consciousness. But Jesus Christ is not a person hiding away within each human subconscious. Jesus Christ breaks into our world through a revelatory historical deed. That reality must always be *directly* proclaimed (proclamatory preaching) to people.

What was true in Kierkegaard's Denmark and what I believe may also be true of our own culture is that the information about Jesus has been communicated again and again. All the information is there. What is missing is inner appropriation: conversion! That cannot be brought about by supplying in direct fashion more layers of information.

The text for Kierkegaard's method was 1 John 2:21, "I write to you, not because you do not know the truth, but because you know it. . . . " Knowing about the truth, however, is not knowing the truth as the inner dynamic of one's own existence. Kierkegaard sought to be a *midwife* delivering information into reality. He was not interested in adding more information to people's existence. The illustration of the sufficiency of information had to be shattered. Kierkegaard, therefore stated his goal succinctly. His method was to help people stand alone with the help of another.

"To stand alone—with another's help." "To stand alone": that was the goal, not dependent on SK or clergy or institution, but before God to have the inwardness of faith. . . . "With another's help": that was SK's task, delicate and difficult, for not only did the illusions have to be shattered, but this had to be done so as not to create disciples . . . around himself.[25]

In this approach Kierkegaard had ultimate respect for the privacy of the listener. He did not wish to thunder directly into their ears. He hoped to indirectly elicit the decision of faith.

As SK put it, the indirect approach "shyly withdraws (for love is always shy) so as not to witness the admission which he makes to himself alone before God—that he has lived hitherto in an illusion." And finally, the listener is permitted room to make the decision about his own existence. That decision is the act which is the end and goal of all SK's art.[26]

Craddock's own word for this method of communication is "overhearing." He derives that from the manner in which Kierkegaard formulated his whole theory and understanding of indirect communication. One day Kirkegaard *overheard* a grandfather talking to his grandson at the grave of the one who had been his son, the boy's father. The grandfather spoke of life and death and eternity. Kierkegaard overheard the whole conversation and was immensely moved. Overhearing the conversation gave Kierkegaard the *distance* he needed in order to *participate* deeply in the event. (Distances enables participation!) Indirect communication, says Craddock, is a kind of overhearing.

The gospel of Jesus Christ upsets all our conventional wisdom. A God who loves sinners? A God-made-flesh who dwelt among us? A God who dies that I ("chief of sinners") might live? A God who in Jesus has no use for the "religious" people of his day? God on a cross? How do we communicate the incredibility of this good news to people? It is by no means an easy task. People come to our pews with their minds full of conventional wisdom. How are we as preachers going to slip the folly of the gospel past the conventional wisdom that clogs up the best of minds to the realities of Jesus Christ? If you have done any field testing on your congregation at all you know that they tend to hear what they are attuned to hear. It is a consumate shock, at times, to find out what people "heard" us saying when we thought we had been so clear about this gospel business. We preached a gospel of good news for sinners. They heard a reaffirmation of the fact that their good lives and religiosity were quite good enough for God after all. "Of course God loves people like us."

How do we get around this conventional wisdom? How do we communicate the gospel in such a situation? I am increasingly convinced that one way we can break through the grid of conventional wisdom that confronts us is by the path of indirection, by the way of story, by making an end-run around the left-hemisphere of the brain. Robert Ornstein thinks that this is precisely one of the functions of storytelling in cultures that seek constantly to break through conventional wisdom.

> The storyteller himself is one of the most important elements in these traditions, in using language to make an "end run around the verbal intellect," to affect a mode of consciousness not reached by the normal verbal intellectual apparatus.[27]

Jesus' parables may function in exactly this way. They are ordinary stories told in ordinary language but they pack a wallop. They shock the hearer out of conventional wisdom into the wise foolishness of what the kingdom of God is like.

> He (Jesus) suggests rather than spells out. He evokes rather than explains. He catches by surprise. . . . He tells stories. He speaks in parables, and though we have approached these parables reverentially all these many years and have heard them expounded as grave and reverent vehicles of holy truth, I suspect that many if not all of them were originally not grave at all but were antic, comic, often more than just a little shocking. . . . It seems to me that more often than not the parables can be read as high and holy jokes about God and about man and about the Gospel itself as the highest and holiest joke of them all.

> Is it possible, I wonder, to say that it is only when you hear the Gospel as a wild and marvelous joke that you really hear it at all? . . . Heard as a joke—high and unbidden and ringing with laughter—it can only be God's thing.[28]

> A large part of the power of the parable is that you do not see it coming. Parable is blind side story-telling.[29]

Indirect communication comes at us "slant." It catches us by surprise. In the surprise, in the catch of the breath, conventional wisdom falls. New wisdom that is old foolishness, that is, the gospel, breaks through. That at least is the hope. In proclamatory preaching words were released from the text and hurled *directly* into the world of the hearer. "Bring forth the best robe and put it on him." "Come to me all who labor and are heavy laden. I will give you rest." These words of the text become, in proclamatory preaching, words of *direct* address to the congregation.

Stories, however, work by *indirection*. The word from the text is *overheard* in another context. As the hearer I overhear words like "Bring forth the best robe . . ." in the context of a story. The words enter my consciousness *indirectly*. If the story in which I hear these words spoken is powerful enough to involve me in its inner life then I will "overhear" these words as words addressed to me. You, the preacher, didn't tell me they were meant for me. I figured that out! I was involved in the story. When the climax came I was there. Eucatastrophe!

5. *Story preaching is open-ended.*

I had a student in the Doctor of Ministry program interested in studying the theory and working at the practice of story preaching. Our agreement for his final project was that he would preach three story sermons in his congregation, gather feedback from them and submit both the sermons and the feedback to me. The first two sermons were stories of sorts but there was no open-endedness. The "point" of the story was obvious. The people who responded to the sermons all got the point he was trying to make.

In his last sermon he told a story without explanation; "the story was the preaching itself." He told the story and he re-told the story of the text. The congregation was left hanging. The response of the people to this story was totally different. Their responses were anything but uniform! Each person had completed the sermon for him/herself in a way that fit their own life situation. They made their own applications. Rather than getting "his" point, they completed the sermon in such a way that something meaningful happened in their own experience of hearing and reflecting. The open-endedness of story preaching is inevitable if participation and involvement of the listener is a fundamental goal!

But what if we tell a radically open-ended story (a story with no explanation) and they don't get the point? Or suppose they get the wrong point? Those are the questions most often asked of me about story preaching. My response to these kinds of questions is to ask a counter question. "Are you sure they get the point of your conventional sermons?" We fool ourselves if we think everyone gets the point of didactic or even proclamatory preaching. Unfortunately this fact is easy to document. Let people fill out some form of questionnaire on your sermons indicating what they think your main points were. Very, very few of us come out smelling like a rose in the light of such questionnaires. We might have thought we made our point clearly and effectively. The responses too often prove otherwise. In other words, we kid ourselves if we think our normal preaching procedures are *closed off* in their meaning. People will hear what they will hear. Some things, especially gospel things, are just not easily heard!

Story preaching can be done in such a way that "the story is the preaching itself." We don't need to finish off our stories by saying, "The point of this story is. . . ." If we don't add an explanatory footnote we have left our sermon open-ended. Those open ends, however, live within the limitations of a number of boundaries. The stories we tell have a context. They are limited by a number of factors which provide the interpretive clues for the hearer. We tell them, first of all, in the context of a church service. Everyone in the audience knows that our story is not about how to build an automobile or how to succeed in business or how to fill out an income tax form. The story is told in a church. It is a story immediately influenced, therefore, by all that worship means to the hearer. It is a story told in a Christian context!

Furthermore, our story lives in some kind of integral relationship to the text of Scripture that is read for the day. I presuppose that story preaching is firmly anchored in biblical texts. I presuppose that the story of Jesus is *the* story of the human race that embraces all our stories. The hymns we sing and the prayers we pray also surround the story and provide further clues for interpretation. A story sermon lives in a definite context of worship and text and hymns and prayers. The context closes off many open ends even though it is the listener and not the preacher who makes the connections.

Story preaching does not *have* to be without explanation. I have already said that. The sermons I present in the next chapter will show that. But they *can* be without explanation. They can be radically open-ended. A radically open-ended sermon is something like a joke: you either get it or you don't. Explanation kills it.

Theologically I think that the analog to the open-endedness of story preaching is the Holy Spirit. Our stories are given birth by particular texts of Scripture. They are set within the context of the worshiping community. The Holy Spirit works through the instrumentality of biblical text and the gathered people of God. Could we not think of open-endedness as an openness precisely to the work of the Spirit? Where everything is not spelled out in exact detail perhaps the Spirit of God can move and work with our stories in order that those who hear may hear what it is that God wishes addressed to them. Open-endedness may well enable the Spirit to speak different words out of the foundational text to different people. I will go on telling stories in the confident hope that precisely that may happen.

But it *is* risky! Preaching in story form, preaching open-endedly, means we give up final control over the content of what we preach. We cannot know how the people sitting in our pews will complete our story and apply it to their own life. Story preaching, therefore, is a faith venture. The preacher dares to believe that the Spirit of God may move even where he or she has given up control. Risky indeed!

6. *Faith is evoked by the eucatastrophic experience.*

Preaching and faith have everything to do with each other. "Faith comes from what is heard, and what is heard comes by the preaching of Christ" (Rom. 10:17). One can run that correlation both ways. On the one hand, our understanding of what faith is will shape the style and type of our preaching. On the other hand, our preaching of Christ has much to do with the kind of faith that is engendered in the hearer.

In the first chapter I argued that didactic preaching will tend to engender a *cognitive* faith. The faithful hearer believes that the ideas heard are true ideas. Proclamatory preaching, our second type, tends to engender faith as trust in the living Word of God as it addresses us in the midst of our human situation. God's Word has announced, via the instrumentality of preaching, a new reality for our lives. Faith believes that this announced reality is for real; it is the new reality of our life.

The faith engendered by story preaching is similar in nature to what we have just described. What differs is the way in which this faith in the powerful, life-giving, promissory Word of God is brought to birth. That Word comes to its hearers *indirectly rather than directly.* God's Word is overheard!

I hear a story in which a "good turn," a eucatastrophe, occurs.

> If story is the vehicle of reality rather than either thought or sensation, then recognition, not cognition, is the way we grasp reality, or are grasped by it." [30]

In other words, a story does not teach me things I ought to know (cognition). Rather it is in the story that I *recognize* myself! Not knowledge but *acknowledgment* is the way of story. In a story that is full of the gospel, full of "good turns," full of eucatastrophe I recognize and acknowledge that this eucatastrophe evokes recognition and acknowledgment. The story points to the great eucatastrophe of the human race (Jesus) and in so doing embraces me (my story) within its horizon. "Oh!", I say. "That's me in the story. It's my life that has been (good) turned around."

Stories evoke. They evoke recognition and acknowledgment. Stories that pass on the eucatastrophe of the gospel of our Lord Jesus Christ evoke the firm belief that what has happened has happened for me. Faith comes by *overhearing!*

Some Suggestions for the Craft of Story Preaching

Before presenting some of my own efforts at Story Preaching I would like to make some practical suggestions regarding the creation of a sermon-in-story. I want to present some suggestions I have worked out through trial and error, but first let me say a word about the arts of *creating* and *telling* stories. These skills are not included in many seminary curricula. Most of us are novices in these areas. If you choose to make story preaching a part of your preaching agenda it may be well for you to pay a visit to your nearest public library and check out some basic works on writing stories, and telling stories. You can grasp the essential components of these tasks rather quickly though the refining of such skills comes only through practice and hard work.

Having visited our public library and having read some basic books in the areas of creating and telling stories it appears to me that the essential elements of these tasks can be set forth succinctly. In order to create a story the first thing we must do is to have a fairly clear idea of what we want the story to accomplish. With that idea in place we can proceed to outline the potential story (an outline which may experience much change during the actual process of writing) sketching out and setting of the story, the chief characters, the problem (plot) that will need resolution, the episodes of the story itself and the conclusion toward which we are striving.

Beginnings and endings are of fundamental importance in this story-forming process. We all remember the beginning and ending of those stories that we read and heard as children: "Once upon a time . . . and they lived happily ever after." "Once upon a time," is a beginning which gets us immediately into the story. The completion of that sentence will take us directly into the story. That's important. Stories should begin quickly. In the first couple of minutes the listener ought to know the setting, the time and place of the story, and the conflict or problem to be resolved. This is necessary in order to invite the listener into immediate participation in the story.

Once the listener knows the setting, the characters and the plot, that listener is ready for the main action of the story. The central section of the story chronicles this action. It is in detailing the action of the story that we as storytellers need to learn the art of *conversation* and *description* in order to move the story from its inception through the life of the people and the plot towards the story's climactic moment. Once the action reaches its climax a story normally moves to a rather quick conclusion.

A beginning which gets us directly acquainted with the people and the setting, a stating of the problem (plot), the action that carries that plot along toward its climax and a quick movement toward the conclusion: that's one way to describe the basic structure of a story.

Storytelling, as I read about it, is also composed of some basic ingredients that we recognize as somewhat obvious when we hear them set forth. Storytelling, for example, should be done freely and spontaneously. Stories should not be read nor should they bear the marks of a kind of wooden memorization process. The words we use and the way we use them with the marvelous instrument of the human voice are the most important ingredients in the art of storytelling. Our facial expressions, the movement of our eyes (the focal point of the listener's gaze) and the gestures of our hands are also important aspects of this art.

These suggestions on the art of creating and telling a story I have picked up in my reading on the subject. You can add to these basic ingredients through your own research. Let me now turn to some suggestions that come out of my own experiments in creating stories for preaching. The list that I give is not intended to be exhaustive by any means. Story Preaching awaits your imagination for its fulfillment. Some of these suggestions are of more import than others but they are presented here in random fashion.

1. Always begin with a text. Story Preaching must be anchored firmly to a given text(s) of Scripture. Our interest is not in the creative potential of our own storytelling ability. We are concerned with recasting a biblical text so that it might come alive for our hearers in new ways. Use the text creatively throughout the entire worship service and throughout your sermon. Sing hymns that highlight that text. Use prayers that grow out of its images. Read the text at the beginning or in the middle or at the end (or all three) of the story you tell. *Your story is told in the service of the text;* the text is not the excuse/springboard for your story.

2. Flannery O'Connor is reported to have said that grace can only be portrayed in the lives of real people. I agree. The best story preaching uses stories that involve people that our hearers can identify with. The creative imagination of the storyteller is tempted to leap out into uncharted worlds of elves, centaurs and the like.

The incarnation stands as the clue to our storytelling. God became a human being to save human beings. We have not been rescued *from* our humanity but *for* our humanity. God as human has restored us to full humanity. The danger of stories involving other species is that they so often have one specie "saving" another (monkeys saving elephants, e.g.). Such stories fundamentally deny the incarnation and create immediate possibilities of Gnostic and docetic heresies arising afresh in our midst. "People" your stories! The story of our salvation in Jesus

Christ is a people-to-people story. The humanly incarnate character of the Jesus story ought not be violated.

3. Your autobiography can be an effective method of story preaching. The extreme popularity of religious auto-biographies among lay people ought to indicate the truth of this. In many Christian traditions, from the stories of the saints in Roman Catholicism to the tent-meeting testi-mony, autobiographies have played an important role.

> The way to the self, as Arendt suggests, goes through indirection, through the story of the self in speech and action as a metaphor or parable of the self. We cannot look at the self directly, for like mercury it squirts away from our sight; but we can evoke the self through a similitude of it, through the metaphor we call auto-biography. That is what autobiography is—a likeness or metaphor of the self . . . what we want from other auto-biographies is finally self-knowledge.[31]

This is the *possibility* of autobiographical preaching. Our hearers may be enabled to see themselves by indirec-tion. This is so because autobiography has the potential for creating distance and, as we have seen, distance may enable participation. It is safe for people to listen to you share with them the elements of your own life story. They can laugh at you, cry with you, disagree with you, etc. They have the space to do that. That space is what is important about autobiography. They can take you or leave you! They may finally identify strongly with your story and see themselves in your faith struggles. If they choose to participate in your story that is a decision freely made. You haven't forced it upon them.

For these reasons I highly recommend the autobio-graphical format when you need to deal with highly charged social, political and ethical issues. You can in-vite your audience into your own struggle with the issue at hand. You can invite them to hear how you have resolved the issue for yourself. They can hear you go through your thinking process on the matter. That is a radically different psychological approach than engaging your congregation in a sermon where you simply tell them what is right on a given issue. When you tell them the "way of the matter" they have no space for disagreement. If they disagree they have to fight. The autobiographical presentation allows people to follow you through your process and agree with you or to say to themselves, "That's not the conclusion I would have reached." It makes a world of difference to the hearer whether controversial issues are presented as, "I've been thinking this thing through and here are my conclusions," rather than, "The Lord and I say. . . ."

Autobiographical preaching was almost always totally discouraged in the tradition in which I was trained. "Don't talk about yourself!" I have come to see that autobiographical story preaching, done well, can be a helpful way of communicating the gospel. But there are problems. Obviously we can talk about ourselves too much. Even more problematic, when we talk about ourselves we may create a halo effect. Things always come out right in our story. That's just what must be avoided. Autobiography should only be used in the service of the gospel; never in the service of the self. That means that in my stories of self I come off as the sinner, not the saint. God's grace covers me, even me! That's the reality of your life you want people ultimately to identify with. God's grace! Even *me*.

4. Know the difference between allegory and parable when you create a story. An allegory is a story that has several points of correspondence to things already known

by the congregation. They know as they listen that the woman in your story is Mary, the baby is Jesus, the airplane is the donkey, the Hilton Hotel is the inn, etc. The art of listening to an allegory is the art of figuring out what each part of the story corresponds to. Allegory contains few surprises!

My own counsel is to create parables rather than allegories in story preaching. If you have not tried it before, you will find, I think, that your first efforts at creating stories are by nature allegorical. Parables, on the other hand, strive toward a single conclusion. They seek to capture the central experience of the text. Parabolic stories, as I would understand them, have somewhat of a surprise or shock ending. The hearer doesn't really know how it is going to end and it is only when it ends that the hearer begins to make connections between the story and the text for the day. The hearer does not hear the story by decoding the details of the new story into the known details of the familiar story (text). Rather, the story is heard through to the singular, often shocking, ending. "What is going to happen?" the listener wonders. "How will this end?" That's a different kind of listening than "allegorical" listening which wonders, "The woman must be Mary, the baby must be Jesus. . . ." If you choose to attempt some story preaching I cannot urge it upon you strongly enough that you learn how to tell stories that strive, insofar as that is possible, toward a *single conclusion*.

5. Visual clues may enhance greater listener participation in your story. For me the classic paradigm of this approach is an old television series called *Mission Impossible*. At the beginning of each program the audience saw and heard the plot, the people who would be involved in solving the plot and some of the means (a false passport,

a clown's disguise, a car with no engine) whereby the plot would be solved. With these clues in mind the viewer watched the program, constantly wondering when and for what purpose the people and the means would be used. The clues invited and secured audience participation.

Let us suppose that your text is John 10:1-8 and you wish to tell a story that captures for your people the heart of what it is to experience Jesus as the Good Shepherd. During the opening hymn you can have someone bring to the front of the sanctuary a shepherd's staff, an old coat-like garment, and a primitive slingshot. Just set it down. No explanation. But everyone knows that somehow, some-where, these visual clues are going to be used. They begin to participate from the very beginning in wondering what these clues lead to. They will anticipate the sermon (story) in the hope of resolving the suspense of imagina-tion that has been created.

We have here the makings of a very cool (remember McLuhan's definition) worship event. Visual clues, your shepherd story, the John 10 text, good use of Psalm 23 and hymns like "Savior, Like a Shepherd Lead Us" pro-vide the images to engage the members of the congrega-tion. Ultimately they must participate and put all of the pieces together. Hopefully, when they leave the sanctuary they will have discovered, in the midst of the worship col-lage, the reality of Jesus as the one who tends and cares for their human life and existence.

6. Create situations for the "overhearing" of the gospel. (Remember Søren Kierkegaard and Fred Craddock.) Children's sermons are a classic example of overhearing. Adults can eavesdrop freely on your conversation with the kids. They are safely removed from the dialog. Why is it then that these adults most often like the children's

sermon the best? I don't know how many times I've heard that sentiment expressed. Craddock may be right: distance enables participation!

I must admit that Craddock's "overhearing" theory has given me a new perspective on children's sermons. It seems to me that a children's sermon can best be defined as a sermon that the adults can understand. We take risks with children's sermons. We even tell stories. The adults love it! There's a message there for all preachers. Sermons for adults ought to be as easy to understand as sermons for children.

We might understand that a sermon for children is a marvelous occasion for adult overhearing. Children's sermons speak to children of all ages. They should not be divorced from the sermon of the day as a totally separate entity. Simple and sprightly communication with children must not be the pretext for complex and boring communication with adults. Let the children's sermon be part of the whole sermon configuration for the day. In other words, part of our sermon on a given day is addressed to a particular segment of the congregation (the children) in a particular place in the church building. That part of your *one* sermon, however, will be *overheard* by all in attendance.

Overhearing actually happens quite often in preaching. At a funeral, words of comfort addressed to the family are overheard by all present in a deeply meaningful way. Mother's Day sermons and confirmation sermons are also overheard. We can create other "overhearing" contexts. The congregation can overhear us speak to God. They can overhear a dialog we construct in a story. They can overhear the dialog of the people in the text as they struggle with God. Many forms of dialog can be the occasion of overhearing.

I overheard a sermon once that was a family dialog. The family was on a camping vacation and Sunday rolled around. Each member of the family expressed his or her opinion on whether or not they should attend church. We, the congregation, overheard a variety of viewpoints. The preacher made no conclusions. All of us overhearers knew where the truth of the matter was. The story was the preaching itself!

7. A simple way to begin story preaching is by creating stories that parallel the biblical text and letting the congregation make the connections between text and story. I tried this one summer with Bible school children. Each day I read to them a parable of Jesus. Then I told them a story about Peter (it was at St. Peter's Church) in which I sought to recast the parable in the language and people of their own world. When I finished I asked them what connections they could make between the two stories. The children always made the right connections.

8. The use of silence can be an effective way to involve people in your sermon. The silence need not be part of a story. My concern here is with the aspect of participation which is such an important part of sermon listening and which story preaching seeks to encourage. I once preached on the text in 2 Timothy 1:3-7 where Paul says to Timothy: "I am reminded of your sincere faith, a faith that dwelt first in your grandmother Lois and your mother Eunice and now, I am sure, dwells in you" (v. 5). I commented on the striking fact that when Paul thought of Timothy's faith he thought at once of Timothy's grandmother! He thought of Lois' faith. Lois was Timothy's "gospel grandmother." None of us come to faith in Jesus Christ alone. We all have "gospel grandmothers." I invited the members of the congregation to think of those people

who were for them "gospel grandmothers." I left a time of silence for them to ponder this vital part of their Christian life.

After the sermon many people talked to me. What they said, however, was different from the normal post-sermon interchange. Not one person said to me, "I liked your sermon, pastor," or "Good sermon," or anything even remotely akin to that. What they did say was, "You know who I thought of. . . ." And they told me. The silence had given them permission and space to reflect on their particular niche and their particular connections within God's grand communion of saints.

9. Biblical texts should be meditated on in the light of stories we know from literature, theater, cinema, TV, music, and human life. I am going to call this way of thinking about the text *vertical exegesis*. The type of exegesis that we normally do is a kind of *horizontal exegesis*. Horizontal exegesis asks temporal questions of a text. What lies behind this text? What did this text mean in its original time and setting? What does the history of interpretation of this text reveal?

Vertical exegesis has another purpose. It thinks about a given text in relation to other stories that you know. The stories you know may be anything from stories from antiquity to the stories of the people in a given parish. Are there other stories that have overtones or similarities or consonances with this text before you? Quite often we will discover stories with similarities to the text. They may be stories we may set parallel to the biblical text for listener reflection. They may be stories that are well known to people containing a thrust or message that is the opposite of the text. Set in tandem with the biblical text these opposite stories may jar our listeners into hearing what the text says. Remembered stories might actually provide us with our entire sermon for the day!

Vertical exegesis searches time and memory for existent stories which may be useful in bringing the text to life. Story preaching does not require that we always create our own stories. We may not be gifted in that way. Stories do exist, however, that may be used in relation to the given biblical text for the day. In this way we can invite the great storytellers of the ages into our pulpits. But it is not only the great storytellers that can be of help. The community in which you live, whatever its size, is full of people with stories and full of the stories of people. This aspect of vertical exegesis does its homework in pastoral calling and visitation. There are living stories all around you. Just be careful to respect the privacy of these living stories if you bring them into your pulpit. A simple change of name, location, and gender is all that it takes. Surely the best preaching we do is that preaching where text (horizontal exegesis) and people (vertical exegesis) meet in creative encounter.

10. Try it! Experiment! Maybe one part of your sermon some Sunday can be in story form. Use the overhearing format of the so-called children's sermon as trial ground. Story preaching is not easy. It's hard work. It's not an every Sunday preaching type for most preachers or for most congregations. It might not even be a once-a-month practice. But, who knows, it could become that. You won't know unless you try. You'll need some forum of feedback to find out what is happening in your story attempts. You'll need ways to help your congregation understand what it is and why it is that you are abandoning the familiar didactic sermon. And yet, with maximal congrega-

tional patience and earnest endeavor on your part, story preaching may just not be your style. So be it.

I don't know everything there is to know about story preaching. Far from it! I'm still experimenting with various possibilities. My experiments constantly give me courage to try different story formats. I find that story preaching only happens in the doing. I can't sit in my study with my completed sermon before me and say, "I know how this will turn out." What I think may bomb might turn out very well and vice-versa. I'm not going to quite experimenting. I hope you'll join me with your experiments. We have a great story to tell. It is the greatest story ever told! I think it's worth all the effort it takes on our part to be about the business of telling the story.

Notes

1. Frederick Buechner, *Telling the Truth: The Gospel as Tragedy, Comedy, and Fairy Tale* (New York: Harper & Row, 1977).
2. Ibid., 91.
3. Ibid., 92, 95-96.
4. A partial listing of theological works which have dealt with story in one form or another would include the following:
   Harvey Cox, *The Seduction of the Spirit*
   John Dominic Crossan, *The Dark Interval*
   Sam Keen, *To a Dancing God* and *Telling Your Story*
   Michael Novak, *Ascent of the Mountain, Flight of the Dove*
   Robert Roth, *Story and Reality*
   Sallie TeSelle, *Speaking in Parables*
   James Wiggins, ed., *Religion as Story*
   Amos Wilder, *Theopoetic*
5. James Wiggins, "Within and Without Stories," in *Religion as Story*, James Wiggins, ed. (New York: Harper & Row, 1975) 3-4.
6. Amos Wilder, *Early Christian Rhetoric: The Language of the Gospel* (Cambridge: Harvard University Press, 1971), 43.

7. Robert E. Ornstein, *The Psychology of Consciousness* (New York: Viking, 1972).

8. Ibid., x.

9. Wayne Lucht, "Teaching Religion to Both Sides of the Brain, *Interaction*, (December, 1976) 14-15.

10. Ornstein, *Psychology*, 51-53.

11. Wilder, *Early Christian Rhetoric*, 126-127.

12. James M. Reese, *Preaching God's Burning Word* (Collegeville: Liturgical Press, 1975), 98-99.

13. Sallie TeSelle, *Speaking in Parables* (Philadelphia: Fortress, 1975), 43.

14. John Dominic Crossan, *In Parables* (New York: Harper & Row, 1973) 13.

15. One of the finest summaries of the work that has been done on the parables in recent years is by Norman Perrin, *Jesus and the Language of the Kingdom* (Philadelphia: Fortress, 1976).

16. Wilder, *Early Christian Rhetoric*, 72, 84.

17. Dan Otto Via, Jr., *The Parables* (Philadelphia: Fortress, 1967) 73-74, 78.

18. Crossan, *In Parables*, 20-21.

19. J. R. R. Tolkien, "On Fairy-Stories," in *Essays Presented to Charles Williams*, C. S. Lewis, ed. (Grand Rapids: Eerdmans, 1966) 81.

20. Ibid., 83.

21. Fred B. Craddock, *Overhearing the Gospel* (Nashville: Abingdon, 1978) 118.

22. Quoted in ibid., 9.

23. Ibid., 82.

24. Ibid., 83-84.

25. Ibid., 91-92.

26. Ibid., 93.

27. Ornstein, *Psychology*, 172.

28. Buechner, *Telling the Truth*, 62-63, 68.

29. John Shea, *Stories of God: An Unauthorized Biography* (Chicago: Thomas More, 1978) 182.

30. Robert Roth, *Story and Reality* (Grand Rapids: Eerdmans, 1973), 52.

31. TeSelle, *Speaking in Parables*, 149-150.

6

STORY SERMONS

The Lonely Lady
of Blairstown Park

Luke 15:11-24

GEORGE MILLER AND HIS WIFE BEE moved to Blairstown sometime in the mid-1950s. George had been transferred there by his company and, though moving was always an unpleasant task, he and his wife didn't complain because the transfer meant quite a good promotion and a good salary hike to boot. Besides, George liked Blairstown. It was a typical midwestern town.

There were many nice features about it. A peaceful river cut the town in half, providing it with much beauty and recreational pleasure. It was a town full of large, well-kept houses. Blairstown hadn't been swamped with World War II-vintage cracker-box homes.

Besides the river and the houses Blairstown had a smartly scrubbed downtown section and a beautiful city park right near the center of the city. George passed that well-groomed park every day on his way to the office. The park had an abundance of plants and flowers and shrubs and trees. As he daily fixed his eyes on that park George noticed that it had something, perhaps we should say some*one*, else too. Nearly every day he passed the park he noticed an elderly lady sitting or standing or walking in some part of the park.

At first George didn't pay much attention to that lonely creature. She did seem to be there almost every time he passed by. "Probably coincidence," he thought to himself. "Or was it?" He began to pay a little closer attention to the lady of the park. She was certainly a very ordinary looking woman. She was not too tall and not too short; not too fat and not too thin. Just ordinary. What was extraordinary about her was the fact that, weather permitting, she was in that park every day of the year. George began to watch her a bit more carefully. "Who was this woman?" he wondered. "And what is she doing in this park?" It almost seemed to George that she was looking for something or someone. A few times their eyes had met and he had felt an intensity in the gaze of her aging eyes that he could not comprehend.

One day George's curiosity finally got the best of him. He cornered Harold Clark, a Blairstown native, and asked him about this woman that people called, "the lonely lady of Blairstown Park." Harold told George this story:

"Oh, you mean Grace. Grace Simon. Yeah, she's spent lots of time in that park in recent years. She's a pretty lonely old soul, Grace is. Her husband, Tom, died when their children were quite young. Three kids they had. The oldest one, Shirley, runs the furniture store on Main Street. Steve, he's the youngest son, runs Simon Funeral Home right next door to the furniture store. Tom Simon started both of those businesses but they divided them up when he died. Since Frank—that was their third child—had died in an automobile accident out west, or so they thought, the one business could be neatly divided between the other two kids. Grace helped them a lot at first. Kids probably couldn't have made it without her. But they don't want her around at all anymore. Kind of a family fight goin' on, if you know what I mean.

"It all started one day when Grace got a letter from Denver, Colorado. Grace wouldn't tell anybody what it was all about but she got all worked up about it. She told Shirley and Steve that she had to go to Colorado right away. Them kids didn't like that one bit. Told her she couldn't go all that way by herself. She begged them to go with her but they refused. She told 'em she'd just have to go alone then. The kids weren't about to pay for that but Grace just wouldn't let up. They finally gave in and gave her money for the long train ride to Denver. So Grace Simon got on the train and headed west.

"Well, as it turned out, the mysterious letter was from Frank. Frank wasn't dead after all. Only he might just as well have been. Turns out he was in jail on several counts of armed robbery. He'd been too ashamed to tell his mother so he had one of his buddies write a letter home saying he had been killed when his car crashed through a bridge and plunged into a river. Even had him send a clipping from a Colorado newspaper that verified the story. Anyhow, for some fool reason, Frank had decided to write and tell his mother the truth. Don't know why he did that. Would've been better for Grace and her family to think he was dead. Nobody wants a jailbird in the family. Lots of people in this town would sure like to wring Frank's neck for that stunt. Bad enough he'd run away from home and do all those rotten things. Let him pay for it. He did it. No use makin' poor Grace Simon suffer 'cause of it. But he did it anyways.

"So Grace went out there. According to the best reports we can piece together there was quite a scene in that prison when Grace Simon and Frank first encountered each other. They led Grace down a long hallway and into a waiting room with lots of other people. A pretty somber bunch I'll bet. Then the guard took Grace into a smaller room just off the waiting room. He told her to wait there —her son would be along soon. She waited for what she said felt like an eternity. Mind you she hadn't seen her son in ten years. Wasn't even sure she'd recognize him. Then she heard the echo of footsteps closing in on the room. She looked up and there he stood in the doorway. As their eyes met they both froze in their tracks. Grace moved first. She wrapped her arms around her son, held him tight, and wept. Cried her eyes out old Grace did. 'We thought you were dead,' she told him over and over again. 'We thought you were dead.'

"When things finally settled down Frank and Grace talked a bit. She visited him several times while she was there. She still goes out there about once a year. Some say he's due for parole any day now. Anyway, she told him right off that when he gets out of that prison he should come home. There's room enough to live with her and he could always be a partner in the family business.

"When she got back to Blairstown she was all excited. 'Frank's alive! My boy's alive. All that accident business was wrong. He's alive I tell ya'. I'll bet I heard her say almost those exact words twenty times myself. She told everybody she knew. Grace was tickled to death. She was about the only one who was, though. Blairstown had never had a native son sent up the river for thirty years for armed robbery before. People around here weren't too keen on the whole idea. Frank might have been alive all right—but he was a crook, a two-bit, good-for-nothin' crook. Folks here didn't have much to say to Grace Simon. I mean what are you supposed to say to a lady like that: 'Gee I'm happy your son is alive—and in jail!'? Doesn't sound so good does it? Most of us just didn't say nothin'. Grace met lots of silence.

"Shirley and Steve weren't silent though. If possible, they were even madder when Grace got home than when she left. It was bad enough that Grace had told Frank to come home at all to disgrace them and their mamma and all of Blairstown. But that she told him that he could be a partner in the family business (!)—that was the last straw. Shirley and Steve were dumbfounded. A *crook* in the family business! Imagine it. In a town this size. It'd never work. Shirley and Steve were right about that. Whole town agreed with them kids on that. No siree. It wouldn't work. Not in Blairstown.

"Grace, of course, didn't look at it that way. Frank was her son too, she argued. He had a right to be back in the family. So Grace, she had her view of the matter and the kids had another. That was the heart of the family feud. The kids, Shirley and Steve, decided to settle it legally. They had a lawyer draw up papers which ruled Frank out of the business altogether. When Grace protested, and protest she did, they told her it was their business. She was never to come in their stores again. Thought that was the unkindest blow of all. After she helped them kids get started and all. Wasn't right of 'em to just throw her out like that even if she had gone off half-cocked on this Frank thing. They don't even invite her over to their homes anymore. Poor Grace. She doesn't even get to see her grandchildren unless they sneak over to the park. Them little ones do that a lot too. Seem to like their grandma real good.

"Well, sir, that's why Grace Simon wanders alone in Blairstown Park. 'The lonely lady of Blairstown Park.' That's what townsfolk call her all right. She's out there waiting and watching. Naturally she's watching for

Frank to come home. But that's not all. You watch her sometime. She's got her eyes on Main Street an awful lot. She's watching for a sign, any sign of recognition or welcome from Shirley and Steve."

George finally interrupted Harold's story. "You'd think she wouldn't want anything to do with those kids," George said. He paused for a moment, reflecting on the story. "What do you suppose Grace would do if those kids did give out any sign of recognition?" he asked Harold.

It was Harold's turn to pause. He scratched his head and thought for a minute. Then he answered. "I think she'd do just what she did with Frank. She'd run down that street, wrap those kids in her arms and cry another ton of joyful tears. Yup. Grace loves those kids. That's just what she would do."

George was silent. Harold's answer was not what he expected to hear. It didn't make any sense to him at all.

(An appropriate hymn may be sung, or a time of silence may be kept at this point.)

There were a lot of people Jesus didn't make any sense to. He certainly didn't make any sense to those proper, respectable people who complained that "This man receives sinners and eats with them" (Luke 15:2). According to St. Luke, when Jesus heard that charge against him, he told the story of the Prodigal Son. The heart of that story is the Prodigal Son's decision to return to his home:

> While he was yet at a distance, his father saw him and had compassion, and ran and embraced him and kissed him. And the son said to him, "Father, I have sinned against heaven and before you; I am no longer worthy to be called your son." But the father said to his servants, "Bring quickly the best robe, and put it on him; and put a ring on his hand, and shoes on his feet; and

bring the fatted calf and kill it, and let us eat and make merry; for this my son was dead, and is alive again; he was lost, and is found."

Luke 15:20-24

The following sermon moves in the direction of Tolkien's fairy-stories. It is a story about an animal world which hopefully invites the hearer (reader) into its life in order to experience eucatastrophe. It is not intended to be allegorical in nature.

I have advised earlier that story sermons should be about people. This sermon contradicts that advice. It does not violate my cautionary word that sermons involving animals may tend to be docetic or gnostic in character. Is this a viable preaching format? I'll let you be the judge.

Bad Sam, the Lost Sheep

Luke 15:3-7

This morning, dear people, we have a rare treat in store for us. We have a guest preacher. It's a little unusual, I admit, but we have a sheep to preach today's sermon. I want to assure you that he comes to us with impeccable credentials. Nothing but the best for First Christian Church. With no further ado, then, let me introduce to you Sam Sheep.

(Pastor makes a gesture of introduction, steps into Sam Sheep's place and continues. . . .)

Thank you Pastor Jensen for that introduction. I am Sam Sheep and I can't tell you how glad I am to have this chance to speak to you this morning. I've always felt that the Bible was a bit unfair to sheep. I trust that you all remember the story of Baalam and his ass from the Old Testament. Baalam's ass spoke to him. Asses speak in the Bible, but there is not one word from a sheep even though we fill up far more of the Bible's pages than they do. It's unfair, I say. But, today at least, I get a chance to change all that.

Now let me see. Where to begin? I suppose we might just as well begin at the beginning. We'll do it. We'll begin with my birth. I must confess to you that there was nothing out of the ordinary about it. Mind you though, I was probably a lot more carefully bred than most of you. You know, we sheep go back a long way in history. In fact, we go back to the very beginnings of the human race. Maybe even before that. I don't know. At any rate, ever since there were people we sheep have been around to assure them the best of wool and, what is considerably less appetizing to me, the best of food.

Now I would like to put in a good word for my brothers and sisters. Our contribution to humankind's happiness should not be overlooked. Our wool has given warmth to peasants and kings for centuries on end. Just think of the important people in history who have shouldered what was shorn from us each springtime! Think of all the shepherds who have tended us. There's some pretty important people there—Abraham, Isaac, Jacob, and David, just to name a few. And poets love us! Get out any anthology of poetry or ask any teacher of literature. They'll tell you how many poems extol the virtue and simplicity of life in our pastures. Pastoral life they call it. Such a life has become the model of life, the very ideal, for many great minds. And, of course, you remember that the song of the angel's announcing the birth of Jesus was sung in our midst. I don't suppose it ever occurs to you to think that there were more sheep in attendance at that celestial concert than there were shepherds. It's not certain how many of my flockmates made it into the stable. You can bet they were there though, and before those Wise Men ever showed up.

But enough generalizing about sheep. It's time, I suppose, to get down to my story. The first thing you should

know about me is that in spite of all the glowing reports
I've given you about sheep, I have never liked being one.
How would you like to be shorn naked each spring? How
would you like it being a good little sheep in the flock
obeying all of the shepherd's commands when you know
full well that the climax of your life is going to be a quick
trip to the market so that you can be slaughtered? Are
you starting to get my point? Frankly I've never understood why you Christians think it's so great to call Jesus
the Good Shepherd. I don't care how "good" he is. If you
are somehow his "sheep" then that means that at some
point you've got to give up your life for his sake. That's
how it is with a shepherd and his sheep.

Well, I didn't like it. But what could I do about it? Once
a sheep, always a sheep. But there was one thing I could
do. I could make life as hard as I knew how for my shepherd. And I did. To tell you the truth, I was a very bad
little sheep. The worst. When our shepherd used to take us
grazing I would always stray as far from the rest of the
flock as I could. You just never knew when that friendly
looking shepherd might be leading you to a shearing, or
worse yet, to the slaughter. So I stayed as far away from
him and the rest of the sheep as I thought safe.

How angry that shepherd would get with me! I don't
know how many days he had to leave the rest of the flock
and look and look and look for me. Boy that was fun. If
you were smart enough, and contrary to our bad press
we sheep are pretty smart creatures, you could always
avoid the shepherd's searching eyes. I should know. I was
the best in the business. He never found me unless I
wanted to be found. I always wandered just far enough
away that I couldn't be found. If danger arose from other
animals, all I had to do was listen very carefully for my
shepherd's voice. A smart sheep always knows his shep-

herd's voice. We can hear it over long distances. So, when danger lurked, I listened very carefully until I heard his voice. Hearing it, I hurried back to the fold as fast as my little legs would take me. The shepherd would be so mad when I would come back. But what could he do?

"Bad Sam" they called me. I don't suppose I have to tell you that I was mighty proud of that nickname. "Bad Sam." I had a reputation. I had something to live up to. It's easy just to go along with the flock. But to stand out, to have a reputation, even if it was a bad reputation, that was something. And I was bad. I was an outcast in many ways, but that was the path I had chosen for myself.

Now, to get to the point of my story. One day I was up to my old tricks. I strayed even further than usual from the shepherd and his nice little sheep. As time went on, you see, I got braver and braver. The badder you get the braver you get. Only this time I went too far. Darkness fell. The sounds of hostile and strange animals howled in my ears. I was scared, I tell you, scared to death. So I did what I always did. I listened. Ever so still, I listened for my shepherd's voice. But try as I might I just couldn't hear it. This time I really had gone too far. As a matter of fact, I was lost. I was lost, I was frightened and I was all alone. I wondered what my shepherd would do about me? "Will he search and search until he finds me out here?" I thought to myself. Suddenly I realized that my reputation was a crushing liability. The shepherd might search out the good sheep. Surely he would. But he wouldn't search for me. Not for me. Not for "Bad Sam."

Minutes turned to hours. The strange sounds of the other creatures were closing in on me. I trembled. "This is the end," I figured. Then I thought I heard a familiar voice off in the distance. I thought I heard my shepherd's voice. He called. I listened. He called again. Again I listened. He called a third time. It was my shepherd. This time I answered with my loudest baaaaaaa. It wasn't long before "Bad Sam" the lost sheep was "Bad Sam" the found sheep.

Now I must confess to you, though I know it will sound presumptuous, that I've always wondered if Jesus knew about me when he told that parable:

> What man of you, having a hundred sheep, if he has lost one of them, does not leave the ninety-nine in the wilderness, and go after the one which is lost, until he finds it? And when he has found it, he lays it on his shoulders, rejoicing. And when he comes home, he calls together his friends and his neighbors, saying to them, "Rejoice with me, for I have found my sheep which was lost." Even so, I tell you, there will be more joy in heaven over one sinner who repents than over ninety-nine righteous persons who need no repentance.
>
> Luke 15:3-7

In the first two sermons presented in this chapter I have tried to create sermons in which the story is the preaching itself. *Most congregations would need some type of background preparation or experience in listening to Story Preaching before such sermons could be effective.*

This sermon, based on Romans 3:19-28, combines both Story and Proclamatory types. The Proclamatory ending serves as a kind of explanation for the story. I have used this sermon in almost precisely the present form in congregations where the story form was new. I offer this sermon to you as the kind of combination of types that is usually necessary in introducing a congregation to Story Preaching.

Martin,
the Justification Addict

Romans 3:19-28

This morning I want to tell you the story of a man named Martin. What you get out of this story will depend a lot on your *participation* in the story. I'd like to ask you to use your imagination and participate, get involved, in this story as best you can. Okay? Here we go!

Martin lived a long ways from this place in a kingdom called Grace. Martin was a nice person. He was attractive and well dressed. You probably would have liked him right off if you had met him. But, having liked him right off the bat, you would have been greatly discouraged to find out that your friend was an addict. Not a television addict. Not a drug addict. Not even an alcohol addict. Martin was a justification addict.

The signs of Martin's strange addiction began to appear when he was just a young boy and blossomed into full maturity in his adult life. The initial symptoms of his addiction began to appear, as far as his parents could remember, when he was in grade school. It appeared at first in what his parents came to call "Yes-But" dialogs.

"Martin," his mother hollered. "Did you knock this cookie jar over and make this mess on the kitchen floor?"

"*Yes, but,*" Martin replied, "someone had just freshly waxed that floor and when I stood up on the chair to reach the cookies, the chair slipped. It's the slippery floor's fault. Not mine!"

"Martin," his father shouted. "Did you leave the TV room in shambles when you went to bed last night?"

"*Yes, but,*" Martin answered, "I was going to clean it and I remembered that you told me I had to go to bed at 8:00 and it was just 8:00 when I thought of it so I thought I had better get to bed like you said."

Martin's parents had lots of these yes-but conversations with him. Martin always had an answer. He always found some way to justify himself.

Martin's teachers got involved in the same kind of yes-but dialogs. "Martin, is it true that you didn't have your math work in on time?"

"Yes, but," Martin replied, "my dad made me stay up late last night and clean up the TV room. Otherwise I would have had it done. I promise."

"Martin. Is this your paper that is so messed up?" his English teacher asked one day.

"Yes, but," Martin said, "it's not my fault. You see my mommy made me clean up the cookie crumbs from the kitchen floor and that was just when I was working on my English paper. You can call her and ask if you don't believe me."

Martin could justify anything and everything. And his justifications were perfectly logical. Martin was never wrong or always right, whichever way we should say it. The problem was that this never-being-wrong and always-being-right got to be an obsession with Martin. When

you've never been wrong, you never want to be wrong
. . . ever!

The truth of the matter, of course, was that Martin was
a very insecure kid. The only security he could seem to
find was the security of always being right. Life for
Martin, therefore, was one round of self-justification
after another. By the way, Martin behaved toward God
the same way he behaved with everyone else. To hear him
tell it, Martin hadn't done anything wrong in the eyes of
God in his entire life.

As Martin grew up the symptoms of his justification
addiction became evident to all who knew him. Once, when
he had just purchased a house, one of his friends (and
there weren't many friends around anymore!) asked him
why he bought it in that part of town. Didn't he know
that property values there were low and everyone pre-
dicted they would go even lower? "Hogwash," Martin
shouted. "I've been to the city planner's office. I studied
the graphs and charts that show the long-range trends for
this community. Believe me. I know what I'm doing. That
house is a great investment. Oh, and by the way," Martin
continued, "I should also point out that I bought this
house because of its superior insulation. Save a lot on fuel
bills. And I bought it on that side of the street because of
the direction of the sun's rays for a possible solar heating
unit."

"You sure you didn't make a mistake?" his friend per-
sisted.

"Mistake! No way. You wait and see. I'll be proved
right on this one."

One day someone just casually asked Martin where he
got what appeared to be a new suit of clothes. "I'm so glad
you asked," Martin said. "I've been watching the sales for
months in order to get this particular suit. Finally Simon's

had the best sale on it. You won't find this particular suit on sale again at their price anywhere in the world. And this material," Martin went on. "It's the most wrinkle-free stuff ever invented. The style and cut is important, too. Figure it'll be in style a good long time. I really got a good buy. You can count on that."

Martin, the justification addict, struck again!

Then one day he bought a new sports car. His friends who knew anything about sports cars were aghast. "Martin, Martin," they pleaded. "Why did you buy this model? It's a lemon, Martin. Everyone knows that. Wake up, man. You've made a real mistake."

That's all you know about sports cars," Martin sneered back. "I've read all the magazines on this year's models. This one has the best rating. It gets more miles to the gallon, it has more interior size, it's got a faster pick-up, it handles and corners better, it . . ." Martin interrupted his own flow of thought. He thought to himself for a moment. Then Martin the justification addict made a regrettable decision. "Get in," he told his friends. They got in and away Martin went. Up and down the streets he wove through the traffic. Around the corners he sped. He pulled away from stop lights like a maniac. Martin was having the time of his life showing off his new car when the familiar sound of a police siren echoed behind him.

"I'm going to have to ticket you for reckless driving," the policeman said. "You are to appear before the judge at 9:00 Monday morning ready to plead guilty or not guilty to the charge."

Martin's life was shattered. He knew there was only one honest plea he could make and that was guilty. But justification addicts can't plead guilty! They can't even say the word. Martin thought and thought and thought and then he thought some more. There had to be a way out of this. Guilty!!! The word stuck in his throat. What would his friends think? What would his family think? What would God think? Guilty. The word rattled around in his mind and nearly destroyed Martin.

Monday morning came. Martin stood stiffly before the judge. "How do you plead?" the judge inquired. There was a long pause followed by an even longer pause. Finally, in a tiny little voice, one word squeaked out of Martin's mouth: "Guilty." The judge pronounced the sentence. Martin, the justification addict, died on the inside.

The judge broke the silence. "Martin. Where do you live?"

"In the kingdom of Grace, your honor," Martin replied.

"Don't you know," the judge continued, "that the kingdom of Grace was established in order to cure justification addicts? In this kingdom the king does the justifying. Self-justification, as you have discovered, is an addiction that leads people into bondage and slavery to their own sense of righteousness. Listen to me, Martin. Hear me as I speak to you on behalf of the king of the kingdom of Grace. 'You are justified! You are justified in my sight today, tomorrow and forever. These words are true. I, the king of the kingdom of Grace, have spoken them to you.' "

Then Martin went home. When he had entered the courtroom that day a destructive word had been rattling around in his head: Guilty. Now a new phrase occupied Martin's consciousness: You are justified. Words like that can do powerful things to people!

The very next day at work Martin's boss stormed into the office and shouted, "Who turned in this sloppy piece of work?" The office was deathly quiet. Out of the hushed stillness a softly spoken word left Martin's lips. "I did, sir."

That weekend Martin and his wife entertained company at their home. "Where'd you get the TV set?" one of his neighbors asked. Martin told her. "And how much did you pay for it?"

"$450," said Martin. The neighbor lady listened to that figure with unrestrained glee.

"We got one just like it at Shoppers Mart for $400 and it's got a bigger screen than yours."

Martin stiffened. His face turned slightly red. Then he relaxed and said, "Sounds like a good deal to me."

It was round 20, or was it round 30, of Martin's ongoing argument with his wife when Martin said something his wife had never heard him say before. "I think you're right," he said. "I'm sorry. It was my fault."

Martin had been set free. The spell of endless rounds of justification had been broken. Martin was no longer a justification junkie. He had been set free to live a new life in the kingdom of Grace.

I'd like to have you listen to parts of today's text in the light of our Martin story.

> Now we know that whatever the law says it speaks to those who are under the law, so that every mouth may be stopped, and the whole world may be held accountable to God. For no human being will be justified in his sight by works of the law. . . . For there is no distinction; since all have sinned and fall short of the glory of God, they are justified by his grace as a gift, through the redemption which is in Christ Jesus. . . . Then what becomes of our boasting? It is excluded. On what principle? On the principle of works? No, but on the principle of faith. For we hold that a man is justified by faith apart from works of law.
>
> Rom. 3:19-28

"For no human being will be justified in his sight by works of the law. . . ."

I look out on this congregation and you know what I

see? I see a congregation full of Martins and Martinas. I see a congregation full of justification addicts. That's a true description of the human condition. Fortunately you have all been invited and called to live in the kingdom of God's grace! I have a word to speak to you today on behalf of the King of the kingdom of grace. I have a word for you on behalf of the God and Father of our Lord Jesus Christ. The word is this: *You are justified.* The words of the text are true. They are true for you. "You are justified by his grace as a gift. . . ." Justification addicts all: You are free! Go then, and live a life of freedom in the kingdom of God's grace.

7

VARIETY IN PREACHING

SOME PARISHIONERS CAN'T FIGURE OUT what we're trying to do in our preaching task; others may figure it out very quickly and tune us out. A range of other responses to our preaching could also be given. What shall we do about it? That's a very difficult and complex question. I have proposed one solution. As preachers we need to think and re-think the task of preaching and move toward variety in our preaching. I have delineated three types: Didactic Preaching, Proclamatory Preaching, and Story Preaching.

Didactic preaching is the dominant style of preaching in the contemporary American pulpit. That troubles me because didactic preaching does not scratch people where they itch. When I am not feeling well and go to the doctor's office I expect more than an explanation of the things that are wrong in my body. I appreciate the doctor's learning and diagnosis. But I want help! I want the doctor to prescribe something or do something or say something that will alleviate the pain I feel.

I expect much the same from the preacher. I appreciate

the preacher's background and knowledge in setting forth for me the three things about the text that I ought to know. But I want help! Didactic preaching, preaching that simply gives out points and lessons about the text, does not offer that help. It may tell me that there is a helper for people like me, but I am not helped in my present condition. I just know more *about* help than I did when I entered the church that day.

Didactic preaching is problematic! It is especially problematic when that is about the only type of preaching that most people ever hear. I don't wish to be misunderstood. Didactic preaching has its place. There are many things I ought to *learn* in relation to my Christian faith. I need to be taught to understand more fully the meaning of my Baptism and the Eucharist and the nature of Christ and the Trinity. I need help in comprehending the complexity of ethical issues that confront me in this age. How does the Bible speak to these issues? I need to know that. I want to hear sermons that help me understand. But I don't want a complete diet of such sermons. I am more than a mind that needs to be taught. I am a person with a complex network of needs. Didactic preaching leaves unmet many of the human needs touched by the gospel of Jesus Christ. Didactic preaching? Certainly. Didactic preaching as the only type of preaching? Certainly not!

Proclamatory preaching announces that there is help for me. It offers help. A word is thrust into my existence that calls me to believe. "Your sins are forgiven," I hear the preacher proclaim. Not, "Jesus is the One who can forgive sins." That's information; that's a lesson. Rather, "Your sins are forgiven." That's help. Proclamatory preaching seeks to announce and herald forth words that speak healing to many of my complex human needs.

Proclamatory preaching, or something very much like it, is an indispensable style of preaching to complement our more didactic efforts.

If I had to preach every sermon in one format I would preach all proclamatory type sermons. But I don't have to preach all sermons in the same style. It's a good thing. Proclamatory preaching as a steady diet would become quite predictable and, perhaps, meaningless. We can only hear certain words thrust into our human situation so many times ("Your sins are forgiven") before they become clichés.

Proclamatory preaching, therefore, has its own kind of problems. Hermeneutically it certainly can run the risk of snatching words out of their context in order to present them afresh in our time. There is also the danger that the gospel message will lose its anchor in the historical life and ministry of Jesus Christ. Proclamatory preaching, therefore, has its risks. Used as one type of preaching in a variety of preaching formats, however, it offers real possibilities of getting the gospel word of Jesus proclaimed to people in their life situations today. Proclamatory preaching offers help. It does more than teach people that help is available.

Story preaching is related to the helping power of the gospel in still another way. It doesn't *teach* me about help (didactic). It doesn't offer me help *directly* through a word hurled into my existence (proclamatory). Rather I hear a story in which help happens. As a listening participant in the life of the story I recognize that this same sort of help is offered to me. Story Preaching offers the help of the gospel *indirectly*.

Story Preaching is by far the most difficult to master of the three types that I have presented. Not everyone will be able to manage it. I hope you don't decide that in advance of trying it out, however. It will certainly be an uncomfortable experience to try out a story sermon only to find out that your effort falls flat. After two or three attempts your people might say to you, "Forget it, Pastor." You should probably heed their advice. But don't be afraid to try out a type of preaching that might fall flat. It won't be the first sermon you or I or anyone else ever preached that suffered that fate!

Three types of preaching. That's what we've been talking about. At this stage of our dialog together I realize that my work can have two totally different effects on you. You can close the book, put it away and not give it another thought. My book will have been an interesting didactic exercise for you. You learned some things. On the other hand, my work might have the open-ended effect of a story. It's all in your hands now. What you do with it is up to you. If my probes into preaching are going to have any effect on your preaching you will have to try out some of the ideas presented herein. Your participation is required to complete what I have outlined.

I invite you to such participation! The next time you plan to preach study your text carefully. After a careful study of the text make a thumbnail outline of how a sermon on that text might look as a didactic sermon, a proclamatory sermon and as a story sermon. You can check back to the characteristics I have given for each type or glance at my differently conceived sermons on the Prodigal Son to remind yourself of the basic difference in types. Creating these outlines should make it clear to you that *there are a variety of ways you can move from your work with the text* (hermeneutics) *to the shape of your sermon* (homiletics). Enabling you to see that variety from a theological point of view has been the goal of this book.

After you have had some practice at outlining the three

different types of sermons for your own sake, try preaching a type of sermon that you haven't tried before. Try preaching a sermon in each of these types. (As I said in the Introduction this whole process may stimulate you to create types other than those I have presented here.) Get some legitimate form of feedback from your congregation on your trials. Ask the high school speech teacher to listen in and offer a critique. Get the reaction of an English teacher to your efforts at Story preaching. Form a "Response to the Sermon" committee of people whose opinions you trust. You preach. Let them react. What happens from there on is entirely up to you.

Using the three types of preaching we have suggested, there are some guidelines that may be helpful in determining which type of sermon to preach on a given Sunday. Thinking about possible sermon types takes place in at least three contexts. In the first place the type of sermon you choose will depend on the biblical text that is the basis for the sermon. Biblical material that has the literary form of story or narrative should not be forced into a didactic style of preaching. Biblical material that is didactic in character will not lend itself very well to proclamatory preaching. The context of the biblical material which is to be the foundation of the sermon is the first factor that needs to be considered in determining a sermon type.

A second context in which our thinking about sermon types takes place is the context of our worship service. What will be happening in the liturgical service on the Sunday in which this sermon will be preached? Will there be communion? Will there be reception of new members? Is the choir singing several special numbers? Is it Easter Sunday? Christmas? Mother's Day? All of these questions have a bearing on the type (to say nothing of the length!) of the sermon. It is easier, for example, to preach a story sermon on a festival Sunday like Easter or Christmas than at some other times of the year. Why? On Easter Sunday, for example, there are a host of images, symbols and metaphors dancing in people's heads before they ever set foot in the church. Included among those images might be the empty tomb, the angel speaking to the women, lilies, the disciples racing to the grave, resurrection, death, life, hope, the butterfly. A story can connect with one or more of these images quite easily. The mind of the listener is fertile ground on this festal day for making connections between a story and the reality of Easter which they have come to celebrate.

The third context for thinking about sermon types is the larger cultural and political world in which we live. Preaching is not just an intramural affair that has to do with people tucked safely away in a church service. The preacher also has the task of connecting the lives of these tucked-away-worshipers with the wider world in which they live out their lives. There are times when the pressures of the world around us force their way into our sermon preparation. Because of a weighty moral issue that has become part of the public debate we might decide that a didactic sermon on the text for the day is in order. Or it may be that a crisis in our community has raised the consciousness of our congregation to the fragility of life in the context of the human family. We determine, therefore, that a proclamatory sermon ("You are the *children* of God") is in order. Perhaps images of a political campaign or a political crisis fill the news. A story sermon can capture these images quite easily enabling our people to connect God's Word and public crisis in their own way— indirectly.

We live in an age where people's lives are bombarded by the electronic media. This electronic environment constitutes a genuine challenge to church life as we have known it. It will be hard to satisfy the needs of "electric people," of a people massaged by the electronic media, through the predominantly *verbal* worship life that is so characteristic of Protestant worship. The first signs of tension between electric media and verbal worship are already beginning to appear. More and more people are choosing to receive their religious nurture from the electric media of radio and TV in the "sanctuary" of their own homes rather than participating in congregational worship life. A goodly number of people have "transferred their membership" from the Sunday morning fellowship to the *invisible religion* that transpires in their private "house church."

The church's response to this new phenomenon must be wide-ranging. In a work of this kind it is only in place for me to suggest that our preaching styles might need to include a greater variety, might need to approximate the electric experience (Story preaching has the greatest potential here.), in order to stay in touch with this generation. For us to see the need to make the changes necessary to communicate the gospel in different styles in our age puts us in a long and distinguished biblical tradition:

To the Jews I became as a Jew, in order to win Jews; to those under the law I became as one under the law— though not being myself under the law—that I might win those under the law. To those outside the law I became as one outside the law—not being without law toward God but under the law of Christ—that I might win those outside the law. I have become all things to all men, that I might by all means save some. I do it all for the sake of the gospel.

1 Cor. 9:20-23